A Short Shocking History of
Christianity

Wolves
in sheep's
clothing

Phil Hinsley

authorHOUSE

AuthorHouse™
1663 Liberty Drive
Bloomington, IN 47403
www.authorhouse.com
Phone: 833-262-8899

Published by AuthorHouse 02/14/2024

ISBN: 979-8-8230-2247-7 (sc)
ISBN: 979-8-8230-2246-0 (e)

The story of the human race is War. Except for brief and precarious interludes, there has never been peace in the world; and before history began, murderous strife was universal and unending.

Shall we all commit suicide? Winston S. Churchill

Church and state authority were intertwined and fed on each other. The later exclusion of the political background from the making of Christian doctrine can be partly attributed to the strong Platonic influence on early Christian theology. Plato taught that there were eternal truths that could be grasped by an elite and imposed on others.

The Closing of the Western Mind Charles Freeman

Nations cannot be Christian; only individuals can. If Christians can fight, then it cannot be for Christianity, for that is a contradiction of Christ himself.

The Gods of War Meic Pearse

PART 1

For someone like me who gets nervous at the thought of an injection I shiver when reading what people of faith went through at the hands of those who believed that people who disagreed with what was considered orthodoxy deserved death.

Wouldn't it had been better if Jesus had predicted that conditions for all would, over the years, improve and that all people would be respected and there would be no persecution or putting to death for their beliefs. But that's not the world we live in. Our dreams of what the world should be is not reality.

Jesus didn't disguise or hide that reality to his disciples. No promises were given of a long, quiet and safe life. It wasn't for him and it wasn't for his followers. The world hasn't got better and Christianity has played its part in coercion, violence and persecution towards Jews and heretics. Jesus knew that that many would be deceived by those who came in his name but brought a different message – a message quite unlike the one he brought.

Jesus made it clear that taking his message to the world would be hazardous. 'I'm sending you out like sheep among wolves.' Earlier he had told them, 'Watch out for false prophets. They come to you in sheep's clothing, but inwardly they are ferocious wolves.' Jesus again repeated it, 'Go, I am sending you out like lambs among wolves.'

In Paul's farewell message to the Ephesian leaders he said, 'I know that after I leave, savage wolves will come in among you and will not spare the flock. Even from your own number some will arise and distort the truth in order to draw away disciples after them.'

It wasn't long before the wolves bared their teeth. John records in his third letter that 'Diotrephes will have nothing to do with us. So when I come I will call attention to what he is doing, spreading malicious nonsense about us. Not satisfied with that, he refuses to welcome other believers. He also stops those who want to do so and puts them out of the church.'

The much-anticipated return of Jesus never happened as the writers of the New Testament expected and a curtain falls over much of what was occurring. But within a hundred years, the church had evolved from being under Jewish leadership to becoming a Gentile church. A quantum shift had taken place.

What does appear is a surge of antisemitism that promotes putting some distance between the Gentile church and its Jewish members who were still holding on to the traditions and customs of their heritage.

The *Didache*, 'The Lord's Teaching Through the Twelve Apostles' of about AD 100 speaks of holding different fast days; 'Do not let your fasts coincide with those of the hypocrites. They (the Jews) fast on Monday and Thursday, so you should fast on Wednesday and Friday.' According to the list of annual Sabbath days that are recorded in the book of Leviticus there is only one day on which fasting is commanded and that is the Day of Atonement, the fifth of seven annual Sabbaths.

Jesus taught his followers; 'When you fast, do not look sombre as the hypocrites do, for they disfigure their faces to show others they are fasting. Truly I tell you, they have received their reward in full. But when you fast, put oil on your head and wash your face, so it will not be obvious to others that you are fasting, but only to your Father, who is unseen; and your Father, who sees what is done in secret, will reward you.'

The tone and content of the *Didache* bears little comparison to the letters of Paul, Peter and John although many think highly of it as an early example of Christian teaching.

Initially, the early church was persecuted by legalistic Jews who believed that by careful observance of the law, referring to laws that had been added after their return from Babylon and specifically circumcision, instituted at the time of Abraham, which was, in their mind, the way to be righteous before God. Paul, in his letter to the Galatians, wrote, 'For in Christ Jesus neither circumcision nor uncircumcision has any value. The only thing that counts is faith expressing itself through love.'

The book of Acts records that when Paul left Athens and went to Corinth he met a Jew named Aquila, who had recently come from Italy with his wife Priscilla, because Claudius had ordered all Jews to leave Rome. Suetonius referred to this in his *Life of Claudius* 'as the Jews were making constant disturbances at the instigation of Chrestus, he banished them from Rome'.

Ivor J. Davidson writes in volume one of his church histories; 'The Birth of the Church', 'The early second-century self-defining of Christianity took place in part amid a strengthening vilification of Judaism that would have appalled earlier leaders of the Jesus movement. Within a few years, the seeds would be sown that would develop into the shocking traditions of Christian antisemitism, in which the Jews would be blamed directly for the crucifixion of the Messiah and regarded as apostates upon whom God's judgment had justly fallen. Yet alongside all of this there remained in parts of the East significant groups of believers in Jesus who continued to prize their Jewishness highly.'

Davidson goes on to write of more persecutions such as in the summer of 257, when the emperor Valerian initiated a new wave of persecutions. Christians not only had to acknowledge the Roman gods but were also forbidden to assemble for worship or visit Christian cemeteries. The persecutions of Valerian were halted by his successor, Gallienus, in 260 to 261, and a number of Christian churches and cemeteries were restored. For the most, the remainder of the century was relatively calm for Christians. There was a brief threat of trouble under the emperor Aurelian in 274 to 275 when it was decreed that the Sun god was to be worshipped as 'Lord of the Roman Empire.' The church historian Eusebius says that Aurelian changed his mind concerning the oppression of Christians. It was Aurelian that chose December 25 as the birthday of the Sun god, Helios. There is a mosaic showing Christ as Helios or Jesus as the Sun of Righteousness. That date came to be celebrated as the birthday of Jesus sometime between 274 and 336.

In late February 303 Diocletian issued the first in a series of edicts against the Christians. A few months later, the pressure escalated still further. When Diocletian fell ill and retired to his native Dalmatia 'to grow cabbages' as a country gentleman his successor Galerius, who ruled in the East, commanded all citizens in every country and in each city to offer sacrifices publicly and libations. In the spring of 311, Galerius was dying painfully, perhaps from cancer. He issued an edict stating that his persecution of Christians was simply to induce them to return to the religion of their ancestors. Now, he granted the churches an amnesty and permitted freedom of assembly, with the request that they pray for his health. He died a week later.

Maximin quickly gained control of the eastern provinces, and fierce persecution continued in many areas. Meanwhile, Constantine, having defeated the Franks in the north, marched south into Italy to challenge Maxentius, whose presence was an obstacle to his obvious ambition to be sole emperor. His instincts were imperial. He lusted for grandeur, the consolidation of power, and the destruction of opponents; and he demanded from his subjects the servilities of the adoration of the purple, far removed from the Christian ideal of humility.

In October 312, Constantine moved his army through Turin and Verona and set up camp near the Milvian Bridge, north of Rome, which Constantine had replaced with a bridge of boats. It was a disaster. Maxentius' forces broke, the bridge of boats collapsed as his men retreated back over it and Maxentius drowned.

The story that Constantine experienced a vision of the cross prior to battle is in other versions presented as a vision of the pagan sun-god. This deity was certainly of enduring importance to him. The coins he issued in his early years as emperor included images of Sol Invictus, 'the Unconquered Sun,' a cult popular with his troops.

It was natural that the vision should attract legend, for it was a watershed in Christian fortunes. In 313, Constantine met the Eastern emperor Licinius at Milan. They jointly issued an edict granting 'both to Christians and all men' the unrestricted right to 'follow the form of worship each desired.' The edict was not a statement of faith, but a form of divine insurance policy. All cults were now protected, and it was not until 391 that Christians enjoyed a definitive monopoly as the state religion.

On March 7, 321, the first day of the week (Sunday) was proclaimed to be a day of rest, in the cities at least, if not in the villages that toiled to feed them. Constantine called it the venerable day of the Sun. Popular pagan festivals and feasts were slowly absorbed into the Christian calendar. Christmas Day is first referred to in a Roman calendar of 336.

PART 2

The first controversy for the early church was the so-called 'Quartodeciman' dispute concerning the date of Easter. Churches in Asia Minor traditionally observed Easter on the same day of the Jewish Passover – the fourteenth day of the month of Nisan, regardless of which day of the week this date fell, hence the name 'Quartodeciman' (fourteenth). They maintained that they were following the example of the apostle John. In Rome Easter was celebrated on the Sunday following the Jewish Passover. The name Easter did not come into use until much later; in the context of the English church, in the seventh century. The name derives from the Saxon term for the Spring Festival in honour of the pagan goddess of the dawn, Eostre.

The church historian Eusebius tells us that Polycarp of Smyrna travelled to Rome in his old age (in 154 or 155) to discuss with the Roman bishop, Anicetus, a number of matters concerning the observance of Easter, including the question of its date. At this stage, annual observance in Rome was still not the norm, and Anicetus followed the principle assumed by his predecessors – that the Lord's resurrection was celebrated every Sunday rather than just once a year. The meeting between Polycarp and Anicetus produced no agreement, but they parted on good terms and pledged to respect each other's positions.

In the East there seems to have been a determination to retain the fourteenth-day practice. In an influential sermon on the Pascha dating to around 170, bishop Melito of Sardis offered an explanation of how the sacrifice of Christ was the fulfilment of the deliverance typified by the Hebrew Passover. His appeal was to the absolute superiority of Christ over the sacrifices that was commanded in the old, and now obsolete covenant, as the book of Hebrews make clear. Sadly, Melito did not show the continuity between Christianity and Judaism but was an attack on Judaism itself, blaming 'ungrateful Israel' for its crime in failing to recognize the Messiah and in orchestrating his crucifixion. The tone of his rhetoric marked a notably low point in early Christian antisemitism.

A generation after Anicetus had agreed to disagree with his Asian brethren, one of his successors aroused considerable opposition by attempting to impose uniformity of practice not only in Rome but also upon the churches in Asia. Victor, bishop of Rome from about 189 to 199 called for a standardization of the Sunday Pascha observance in all churches and threatened to excommunicate any communities that refused to comply.

Victor was opposed by a senior Asian bishop, Polycrates of Ephesus, and also by Irenaeus who, while keeping to the Roman practice himself, argued that Victor's injunction was an abuse of authority that would needlessly divide the churches. Irenaeus's counsel prevailed, and Victor apparently countermanded his excommunication order. In the long term, the position sponsored by Victor would win out, and the Council of Nicaea in 325 would stipulate that Easter should be celebrated everywhere as a Sunday festival. Quartodeciman believers nevertheless continued to exist in Rome for some time.

The Quartodeciman position was certainly the more ancient practice, but it lost out to sheer force of custom, reinforced by the weight of Rome's authority. Rome regarded its right to impress its views on believers elsewhere and how a determined a forceful bishop could be in asserting such a position. 'It was at Nicaea – the city named for Nike, the goddess of victory' writes James Carroll in his book, 'Constantine's Sword' at the council enshrining the Christian victory, that Constantine, forbidding the observance of Easter at Passover time, declared, 'It is unbecoming that on the holiest of festivals we should follow the customs of the Jews; henceforth let us have nothing in common with this odious people.'

Carroll later goes on to write, '… the church fathers, well into the fourth century, warn against Christian participation in Jewish observances. For centuries, Christians' celebration of Easter coincided exactly with Passover, and their observance of the Sabbath continued to take place on Saturday.'

The role the emperors played in defining church doctrine was to prove enormously important. At that first church council at Nicaea the 200 or 250 bishops were welcomed by Constantine who was dressed in glorious robes and glittering diamonds and would have been the nearest thing to divinity they had ever seen. Much of the heated debate centred on whether Christ had existed eternally or as a later creation. The issue was unresolved until Constantine intervened in an attempt to bring agreement and unity by suggesting that the correct way of describing the relationship between Father and Son was to declare them *homoousios*, 'of one substance.' Constantine's insistence on agreement meant that the *homoousios* formula was accepted – any other theological position was condemned. Almost everyone signed up to it. Arius and two bishops were formally excommunicated and Eusebius of Nicomedia was deposed from being a bishop, apparently after he refused to sign the anathemas at the end of the creed.

Constantine had achieved a consensus in the short term but with a formula that began to dissolve soon afterwards. There were immense philosophical problems in understanding how the two divine personalities related to each other if they were of the same substance but also distinct as Father and Son.

Here is the Nicaea creed:

> We believe in one God Father Almighty
> Maker of all things, Seen and unseen.

And in one Lord Jesus Christ the Son of God, begotten as only begotten of the Father, that is of the substance [*ousia*] of the Father, God from God, Light from Light, true God from true God, begotten not made, consubstantial [*homoousios*] with the Father, through whom all things came into existence, both things in heaven and things on earth: who for us men and for our salvation came down and was incarnate and became man, suffered, and rose again on the third day, ascended into heaven, and is coming to judge the living and the dead.

And in the Holy Spirit.

But those who say 'there was a time when he did not exist', [e.g. Arius and his followers] and 'Before being begotten he did not exist'. and that he came into being from non-existence, or who allege that the Son of God is of another *hypostasis* or *ousia*, or is alterable or changeable, these the Catholic and Apostolic Church condemns.

The assembled bishops had missed their chance to describe any relationship between the Spirit and Father and Son. 'The Creed,' wrote Richard Hanson in his 'The Search for the Christian Doctrine of God' 'was a mine of potential confusion and consequently most unlikely to be a means of ending the Arian controversy'. No one could have imagined that the creed, even when modified at the Council of Constantinople in 381, would become the core of the Christian faith.

In 326, Constantine ordered the execution of his illegitimate son, Crispus. Crispus had proved a worthy commander in his own right and had held a consulship. Later gossip, from pagan sources, supplied the story that Constantine's wife Fausta was jealous of Crispus' preferment and feared that her own legitimate sons would be passed over. So she falsely accused Crispus of trying to rape her. Constantine accepted the story but was so appalled when he learned of the deception that he ordered the drowning of Fausta in a scalding bath. It is also alleged that his mother Helena was involved and one pagan report suggests that she was sent by her confessor on her famous pilgrimage to the

Holy Land as a penance. While there Helena is said to have found the *titulas*, the sign that was attached to the top of the cross, which she also found, as well as the site on which the Holy Sepulchre stands. Eusebius, who travelled with Helena makes no mention of the true cross.

Paul Stephenson writes in his book, 'Constantine,' that 'He was a Herculian Caesar, kinsman of Maximian and Maxentius, who witnessed Apollo and venerated Sol Invictus … Honour was paramount to him, and he legislated his own preferred morality. He was short-tempered and stubborn, vain and narcissistic, as one might expect from a channel for divine grace … Constantine required unity of faith to guarantee the continued favour of his god, the god of victory.'

PART 3

The Nicaea Creed was endorsed by the emperor Theodosius at the Council of Constantinople in 381. He had issued an edict in January 380 to the people of that city:

'... We shall believe in the single deity of the father, the Son and the Holy Spirit under the concept of equal majesty and of the Holy Trinity. We command that persons who follow this rule shall embrace the name of catholic Christians. The rest, however, whom we judge demented and insane, shall carry the infamy of heretical dogmas. Their meeting places shall not receive the name of churches, and they shall be smitten first by divine vengeance, and secondly by the retribution of hostility which we shall assume in accordance with divine judgement.'

Theodosius' adoption of the Nicene faith led to his active and sustained condemnation of alternative views. His immediate concern was to restore order through enforcing unity of belief. Theodosius ordered his civil servants to impose the new faith which was somewhat vague. He used orthodoxy as a focus for loyalty to the empire.

There was little interest in Hebrew writings by now. According to the hectoring sermons being preached by a new generation of intolerant Christian clerics, the Jews were not a people with an ancient wisdom to be learned from; they were instead, like the pagans, the hated enemies of the church. A few years earlier, in Constantinople, a local bishop, John, later named Chrysostomos, 'Golden-mouth,' because of his abilities as a preacher, and traditionally was known as John Chrysostom. He was later ordained at Antioch as a deacon in 381 and then as a priest in 386.

John had said that: 'the synagogue is not only a brothel … it is also a den of robbers and a lodging for wild beasts … a dwelling of demons … a place of idolatry.' Chrysostom's writings would later be reprinted with enthusiasm in Nazi Germany.

The spread of Christianity is a story of forced conversion and government persecution. It is a story in which great works of art are destroyed, buildings are defaced and liberties are removed. It is a story in which those who refused to convert were outlawed and, as the persecution deepened, were hounded and even executed by zealous authorities. The brief and sporadic Roman persecutions of Christians would pale in comparison to what the Christians inflicted on others – not to mention on their own heretics.

From the *Codex Theodosianus* in 386, a law was passed targeting those 'who contend about religion' in public. Such people, his law warned, were the 'disturbers of the peace of the church' and they 'shall pay the penalty of high treason with their lives and blood.'

John Chrysostom, in his 'Against the games and theatres,' said his congregations should hunt down sinners and drive them into the way of salvation as relentlessly as a hunter pursues his prey into nets'. He also encouraged them to spy on each other. Enter each other's homes and pry into each other's affairs. Shun those who don't comply, then report all sinners to him and he would punish them accordingly and if you didn't report them then he would punish you too'.

The legal codes of Justinian, who became emperor in 527, reiterated the suppression of the rights of Jews in civic, economic and religious spheres, and they were subject to continued abuse in their daily lives. Meir Holder, in his 'History of the Jewish People,' writes, 'A height of anti-Semitism was reached during the reign of the Emperor Justinian 1. Not content with the laws that severely restricted the economic life of the Jewish population under his rule, Justinian actively interfered in their religious life as well. He prohibited Torah study and many other *mitzvos* – in particular, recitation of the *Shema*, whose clear declaration of the Oneness of G-d openly contradicted Christian doctrine.'

His determination to restore supremacy and unity to the church was paramount. His law codes, a consolidation of existing Roman law, were issued in the names of the emperor and the Lord Jesus Christ. He put in hand legislation to restrict citizenship to orthodox Christians alone. His laws banned all pagan worship. One law, of about 531, exhorted all pagans to come forward for baptism, prohibited them from teaching and ordered that their children should be forcibly instructed in Christianity.

When one of the legalistic teachers of the law listened to how Jesus had answered a question he asked a question in the hope of trapping Jesus into saying something against the offerings sacrificed in the temple, 'Of all the commandments,' he asked, 'which is the most important?' 'The most important one,' answered Jesus, 'Is this: 'Hear, O Israel: the Lord our God, the Lord is one. Love the Lord your God with all your heart and with all your soul and with all your mind and with all your strength.' The second is this: 'Love your neighbour as yourself.' There is no commandment greater than these.'

The *Shema* that Justinian banned was the great commandment that Jesus repeated to the lawyer. The word *Shema* means hear or listen which is the first word of the great commandment from Deuteronomy 6:4-5. The second commandment is from Leviticus 19:18.

PART 4

On 13 November 354, a son was born to a pagan father and a Christian mother in, what is known today as, Algeria. He was named Augustine. In 396 he became the bishop of Hippo. Doctrinally, Augustine was a faithful devotee of the Nicene tradition. His underlying premise was that there is a single truth that can only be grasped through faith; that human beings are helpless; that God is essentially punitive, ready to send even babies into eternal hell; and that one has a right, even a duty, to burn heretics.

The tensions in the church in Africa forced Augustine to work out how to deal with a group called Donatists. Donatus was a bishop of Carthage from 313-355. Bands of violent Donatist followers roamed Numidia and called themselves 'soldiers of Christ' and fought against Catholic landlords. Augustine stressed the authority of the Catholic Church during this crisis. The Donatists believed that they were the true church and that the Catholics were apostate. Persecution was confirmation, to them, that they were righteous. The only emperor that treated them fairly was Julian (called the Apostate).

Augustine wrote, 'What then does brotherly love do? Does it, because it fears the short-lived furnaces for the few, abandon all to the eternal fires of hell? And does it leave so many to perish everlastingly whom others [i.e. the Donatists] will not permit to live in accordance with the teaching of Christ?' Thus the idea of persecution became embedded in medieval Europe. Burning alive, the traditional Roman punishment for counterfeiting coins, was adopted for those who 'counterfeited' the teachings of Christ.

Augustine became ever more prepared to ask for and justify the use of force to deal with it. Coercion could even be presented as obedience to the Lord's command to 'compel them to come in' Luke 14:23 KJV.

He depicted the fate inflicted on the Donatists as a matter of spiritual discipline, a harsh but necessary infliction laid upon them with a positive end in mind. Sometimes, he argued, punishment and fear might move people to repentance in ways love and patience do not. It was the duty of a good Christian to convert heretics – by force, if necessary. This was a theme to which he returned again and again. Far better a little compulsion in this life, than eternal damnation in the next. People could not always be trusted to know what was good for them.

If, as he believed, the Church was the totality of Christ, and salvation was impossible outside it, then it followed that compelling a person into it was an act of mercy. Augustine wrote of the 'kindly harshness' that the Church should use to make unwilling people give in. Repression and violence were the day-to-day tools of a flawed world to Augustine, and he condoned their use provided that the intention was just.

A new era was opening. To worship another god was no longer to be merely different. It was to err. And those who erred were to be seized, struck and – if necessary – wounded. Above all, they were to be stopped.

'There is nothing wrong,' Celsus had written, 'if each nation observes its own laws of worship.' To many of the most powerful thinkers within the Christian Church, nothing could be more abhorrent.

Whatever the complexities of Augustine's own case against the Donatists, his stance served ever after as an example to which some of the European churches' darker tacticians might appeal, and into the medieval, Reformation, and Counter-Reformation periods legitimacy would be sought for more than a few programs of brutal repression by citing Augustine's moves against the Donatists.

Athanasius, 296-373, shared the same opinion, 'One is not supposed to kill, but killing the enemy in battle is both lawful and praiseworthy.

PART 5

The anti-Jewish predilections of key figures such as Constantine and Athanasius were common of Gentile theologians of the Roman era. Athanasius industriously removed from their teachings of Christ every trace of Judaism, and applied 'Jewishness' to his opponents as a sort of villainous tag to discredit their positions. Gregory of Nyssa also distances the orthodox Christian belief from Jewish monotheism. The real thrust of the Cappadocian doctrine was to differentiate the Christian 'Godhead' which now incorporated Jesus and the Holy Spirit, from the monolithic God worshipped by Jews, radical Arians, and later on, by Muslims, Unitarians and others. Christians who accepted this triune God, distributed over three persons, no longer shared Jehovah with their Jewish forebearers or the Supreme Being with their pagan neighbours, nor could Jews or pagans believe in the same God as that worshipped by the Christians. Doctrinally, this is the point at which Christianity breaks decisively with its parent faith and with other forms of monotheism.

The passionate rejection of the Jewish God by the Church

Fathers continued with the leaders of the Reformation in the 16th century. The explicit and wanton antisemitism that thrived in the Reformation is an often-neglected piece of Protestant history. The Jews, as both an ethnic and religious group, were considered detestable by the most well-known Protestant leaders, and so was any theological insight the Jewish heritage had to offer.

John Calvin reveals his attitude towards the Jews in this way: '[the Jews] rotten and unbending stiffneckedness deserves that they be oppressed unendingly and without measure or end and that they die in their misery without the pity of anyone.'

Martin Luther writes: 'Such a desperate, thoroughly evil, poisonous, and devilish lot are these Jews, who for these fourteen hundred years have been and still are out plague, our pestilence, and our misfortune. What then shall we Christians do with this damned, rejected race of Jews? First, their synagogues should be set on fire, and whatever does not burn up should be covered or spread over with dirt so that no one may ever be able to see a cinder or stone of it. And this ought to be done for the honour of God and of Christianity in order that God may see that we are Christians, and that we have not wittingly tolerated or approved of such public lying, cursing, and blaspheming of his Son and his Christians.

'Second, their homes should likewise be broken down and destroyed. Thirdly, they should be deprived of their prayer-books and Talmuds in which such idolatry, lies, cursing, and blasphemy are taught. Fourthly, their rabbis must be forbidden under threat of death to teach anymore'.

PART 6

The writer of '*Ecclesiastical History of the English People*' The Venerable Bede, 673-735, describes with approval the massacre of a group of heretical Welsh priests 'because they had despised the offer of everlasting salvation' through their obstinacy. Bede first writes of Augustine, 'that man of God, (not Augustine of Hippo but bishop Augustine who was appointed archbishop of the church in England in 597) is said to have answered with a threat that was also a prophecy: if they refused to accept peace with fellow-Christians, they would be forced to accept war at the hands of enemies; and if they refused to preach to the English the way of life, they would eventually suffer at their hands the penalty of death. And by divine judgement, all these things happened as Augustine foretold'.

Then Bede goes on to tell of a battle near Chester, 'Before battle was joined, he (King Ethelfrid) noticed that their (the faithless Britons) priests were assembled apart in a safer place to pray for their soldiers, and he enquired who they were and what they had come there to do. Most of these priests came from the monastery of Bangor ... all of whom supported themselves by manual work. Most of these monks, who had kept a three-day fast, had gathered at the battle, guarded by a certain Brocmail, who was there to protect them from the swords of the barbarians while they were intent on prayer. As soon as King Ethelfrid was informed of their purpose, he said: 'If they are crying to their God against us, they are fighting against us even if they do not bear arms.' He therefore directed his first attack against them, and then destroyed the rest of the accused army ... It is said that of the monks who had come to pray about twelve hundred perished in this battle, and only fifty escaped by flight ... Thus, long after his death, was fulfilled Bishop Augustin's prophecy that the faithless Britons, who had rejected the offer of eternal salvation, would incur the punishment of temporal destruction.'

PART 7

Religion, an ancient Arab saying went, 'is a falcon with which to hunt.' Christians also learned to use their faith as an instrument of war, finding the fierce bird to be immensely adaptable. They flew it against German emperors, French heretics, and Greek schismatics as well as nonbelievers in the Mediterranean and the Baltic; it was to cross the Atlantic and the pacific to add religious zeal to the expansion of empires. It was difficult to control once set loose, and as mastery of the Church slipped in time from clerical hands, it became the creature of kings and parliaments. It was used in the first instance by the pope, and Moslems were its prey. A crowd too large to fit into the cathedral gathered in a sloping field outside Clermont, in central France on November 17, 1095. Pope Urban II told them that the Byzantine emperor was pleading for help in fighting the Seljuk Turks. He told them that it would be a disgrace 'if a race so despicable, degenerate and enslaved by demons' should overcome a Christian people.

The pope himself had, as it were, claimed an authority bolder and more ancient than that of Peter; he was now the successor to Moses, able to command his flock to war. No Christian doctrine of holy war existed before Urban made that speech at Clermont, unless you went back almost seven centuries to the writings of Augustine. The Crusades were not Christian in any sense. Within a few years, the killing – 'coercion' was the technical term used – of non-Catholic heretics as well as nonbelieving Moslems was enshrined in the canon law of the Western Church.

As the Crusaders moved eastwards they murdered Jews in the cities they came to as well as ransacking the countryside for wine, meat and corn. 'If you want to know what was done to the enemies we found in the city, know this,' Raymond of Toulouse wrote to the pope when Jerusalem fell in July 1099, 'that in the portico of Solomon and in his temple, our men rode in the blood of the Saracens up to the knees of their horses.' It was, so the Crusaders believed, a divine slaughter. Before the assault they had been led by priests in barefoot procession around the city walls as a sign of penance.

The old ambivalence at the heart of the Christian faith – the ability of men of conscience to construct ideologies that are in startling contradiction to the common texts found in the Testaments – was laid bare by the massacre. Apologists said that the God of Exodus ordained it. 'The Lord is a man of war,' they quoted. A smaller number stressed the Son and his warning that those who take up the sword shall perish by the sword. 'Christ did not shed his blood for the acquisition of Jerusalem,' Abbot Adam of Perseigne said with revulsion, 'but rather to win and save souls.'

Between the meekness of Christ and the cruelty of the Christian soldier lay a gulf so wide and obvious that it required an explanation. The Western Church looked to Augustine to provide it. It was, he had written, a Christian duty to fight in a just war, provided that it reflected the will of God and not the desires and rashness of men. Moses was following divine commands, he was not savage but obedient, and God, in ordering such things, was not savage but was … striking with awe those who deserved it.' Why should war itself be blamed? 'This is the complaint of the timid mind, not of the religious,' he said. 'Certain wars that must be waged against the violence of those resisting are commanded by God or by a legitimate ruler and are undertaken by the good.'

Priests were to refrain from violence themselves but were free to encourage it in others: 'Priests themselves ought not seize arms in their hands, but it is allowed for them to encourage others to do so for defence against oppressors and to fight the enemies of God.' The sermon at Clermont was now a matter of law, and the Church formally reserved to itself the right to initiate religious war and heretic hunts.

PART 8

In the Times, Saturday October 28 2023, Dominic Sandbrook wrote an article on antisemitism in England. It is worth reading, '… For anybody who doubts that antisemitism is deeply embedded in England's history, the story of Little Hugh of Lincoln, serves as a terrible rebuke. The most famous version comes from the medieval chronicler Matthew Paris, who recorded that in late July 1255, 'the Jews of Lincoln stole a boy called Hugh, who was about eight years old. After shutting him up in a secret chamber, where they fed him on milk and other childish food, they sent to almost all the cities of England in which there were Jews, and summoned some of their sect to be present at a sacrifice to take place at Lincoln.'

Then, according to Paris, Hugh's kidnappers subjected him to a dreadful ritual, in mockery of the suffering of Christ. 'They scourged him till the blood flowed, they crowned him with thorns, mocked him, and spat upon him … and kept gnashing their teeth and calling him Jesus, the false prophet. And after tormenting him in diverse ways they crucified him, and pierced him to the heart with a spear.' And then, wrote Paris, they dismembered his corpse, 'for the purpose of their magic arts'.

The story was a lie, of course. It was the latest iteration of the antisemitic 'blood libel' which had originated a century earlier in Norwich: the claim that every year, England's tiny Jewish population held a secret ritual, in which they ritually murdered a little Christian boy. The pattern was always very similar. A boy went missing; his body was found; rumours spread that the Jews were responsible. The local monks would then set up a shrine. When miracles inevitably followed, thousands of pilgrims would flock to the scene, providing a welcome boost to the local economy. Everybody won. Except, of course for the little boy. And the Jews.

As the story of little Hugh reminds us, the blood libel was not just a cynical marketing plot, but a lie with lethal consequences. When he disappeared in Lincoln, a royal official called John of Lexington arrested a local Jewish man, known as Copin, and questioned him under torture. Then the king, Henry III, arrived in the city and took a personal interest in the case. On his orders, the hapless Copin was dragged through the streets and hanged.

But this was only the beginning. On his return to London, Henry ordered 92 Jews to be rounded up and held in the tower, accused of complicity in the non-existent conspiracy. Eighteen were hanged immediately, having refused to acknowledge the court. The others languished in prison for months before being convicted and sentenced to death, only to be released after an intercession by the king's brother, Richard of Cornwall. Sadly, their names and thoughts are lost, so we can only imagine their sheer confusion, terror and trauma. Historians have often wondered why Henry, a long-serving but relatively ineffectual king, was so quick to believe such flimsy accusations. One answer is that he was chronically short of cash and keen to squeeze the wealthy Jewish community for all their were worth. But another, more troubling explanation is that he was predisposed to think of Jews as murderers and torturers because antisemitism was already so deeply rooted in English society and culture.

Jews had lived in England since the Norman Conquest, though they did so as 'royal serfs', answerable to the crown. At first antisemitism seems to have been relatively mild, but by the 12ᵗʰ century – the age of the first Crusades, in which religious excitement reached fever pitch – the mood had turned ugly. The first blood libel, in Norwich, dates from 1144, and was followed by a rash of similar stories about Jewish child murders.

Worse was to follow. In the winter of 1189-90, as Richard the Lionheart was preparing to embark on the Third Crusade, pogroms broke out in towns across the country. In York, at least a hundred Jewish men, women and children took refuge in the castle, under siege from a furious mob demanding that they submit to Christian baptism. On the orders of their leader, Rabbi Yom Tov, they began to kill themselves; then Yom Tov set fire to the tower, so their bodies would not be mutilated. Only a handful surrendered and agreed to convert. The mob slaughtered them anyway.

Even centuries later, such stories still make for harrowing reading. To many of us, the resurgence of antisemitism in recent years, especially among supposedly high-minded, moralistic people on the liberal wing of the political spectrum, seems a baffling and distressing phenomenon.

But we should face the fact that antisemitism has always had a distinctive British pedigree, from the legend of Little Hugh to the yellow badges imposed by Edward I, and from caricatures such as Shylock and Fagin to the spectacle of people making excuses for Hamas's atrocities earlier this month.

British antisemitism has, of course, evolved over time, from the overtly religious antagonism of the Middle Ages to the explicitly racialised contempt of the Victorians and the reactionary conspiracy theories of the 1920s. But it remains the most potent conspiracy theory in our political and social life, a poison that shames and stains our national conversation … But as the last few weeks have made depressingly clear, we have not travelled as far from the spirit of 1255 as many of us might like to think.'

PART 9

In 1378 a Yorkshireman said that 'Scripture was the highest authority for every Christian and the standard of faith and of all human perfection.' John Wycliffe taught that the word of God was the greatest authority to which a Christian was bound. He also said that the Bible must be translated into English. Those who supported and followed him were called 'Bible men' and 'Lollards.'

He gave a series of lectures at Oxford and stressed the importance of personal faith in Christ. Wycliffe questioned the teachings of the church and the church itself – its doctrines, he said, 'stuffs the people only too effectually with garbage.' He described the pope as a thief, the 'most cursed of dippers and purse-heavers,' who 'vilified, nullified and utterly defaced' the commandments of God.

Wycliffe was sent, by the English government, to Bruges to discuss clerical abuses with papal ambassadors. He called for the confiscation of Church estates and wealth on the grounds of dereliction of spiritual duty which alarmed the English bishops. He had to appear before them and the archbishop at St Paul's in London in 1377. He was protected by the most influential and anticlerical man in the kingdom, John of Gaunt. Rome became involved and Gregory X1 banned Wycliffe in May and sent bulls to the king and the bishops ordering them to imprison him for the heresies which he 'vomits forth from the poisonous confines of his breast.'

Gregory died in March 1378 and Wycliffe was greatly helped by the moral squalor into which the papacy now sank.

There had been two popes, two administrations, and two courts before; but never had there been two popes elected by the same group of cardinals. A Great Schism was born. The loyalties of nations, universities, and religious orders were divided as France, Burgundy, Savoy, Naples, the Spanish kingdoms, and Scotland declared for Clement in Avignon, while England, Germany, Poland, Hungary, and Scandinavia remained with Urban in Rome.

The two popes at once excommunicated each other. Both sides naturally ignored the other's censures. Five cardinals consulted a jurist to see whether insanity could be used as grounds for removing Urban as his manias were running unchecked. But he had them arrested and tortured, ignoring their screams while he walked in a nearby garden reciting his breviary. They were not seen again.

Wycliffe responded with, 'I always knew that the pope had cloven feet, now he has a cloven head.'

Wycliffe found no biblical justification for the dogma of transubstantiation. The doctrine was first taught by a theologian named Paschasius Radbertus in about 831 – as God had implanted Christ in the Virgin Mary, he also created the real Presence of the flesh born of Mary in the

Eucharist. By consuming the Host, the faithful enter into Christ's mystical body, the Church. The mystery of this transubstantiation was confirmed at the Lateran council of 1215.

Bells were rung and candles lit as the Host was elevated at Mass amid whorls of incense, the faithful looking up in devotion to the divine evidence of Christ's sacrifice and their own redemption. Only the priest could celebrate its mysteries, and only he could receive the wine, the laity was denied the chalice.

Wycliffe insisted that 'The consecrated Host we see on the altar is neither Christ nor any part of him but the efficacious sign of him.' On May 17, 1382, Archbishop Courtenay convoked a council at Blackfriars in London to condemn twenty-four of Wycliffe's propositions as 'heretical and erroneous.' Wycliffe was forced to give up his teaching at Oxford and retired to his rectory at Lutterworth in the Midlands. Wycliffe was a nationalist and said, 'There cannot be two temporal sovereigns in one country; either Edward is King or Urban is king. We make our choice. We accept Edward of England and refute Urban of Rome.'

Writing almost entirely in English now, he spurned Latin as the language of ecclesiastical privilege. 'Why may we not write in English the gospel and other things declaring the gospel to the edification of Christian men's souls?'

Wycliffe died of a stroke at Lutterworth on New Years Eve, 1384, some eight years before the translation of the Vulgate in to the English dialect was completed. Although it was largely the work of his followers, he was its inspiration, and its rendering from dusty Latin into vivid prose. It gave the English their first direct contact with the word of God in their own language.

Over thirty years later, on May 4, 1415, a committee appointed by the Council of Constance in Bavaria examined Wycliffe's writings, and condemned them as heretical on 260 counts. His influence in Bohemia had been so great that not only were his books burnt, but his bones were ordered to be dug up and cast out of consecrated grounds. Nothing was done until December 9, 1427 (another author says it was early in 1428). It was ordered that his body and bones were to be exhumed and publicly burnt, and his ashes to be disposed of so that no trace of him should be seen again. They were cast into the River Swift at Lutterworth.

PART 10

Jan Hus of Bohemia was a philosopher and a theological lecturer at the University of Prague. A man of deep religious conviction, he had come to lament the idle days of his youth, when he wasted too much time enjoying himself. As he himself admitted, he had played far too much chess and spent too much money on expensive clothes. The catalyst in his life had been the teachings of the great English church reformer John Wycliffe, the inspiration of the Lollards. Like Wycliffe, Hus was appalled at the sale of indulgences – grants of absolution for one's sins – by the church. Following Wycliffe, he argued that forgiveness should be sought through repentance and atonement, not through the payment of money. He was also appalled by the idea that the pope could command what men should believe, and what they should say they believed, regardless of how God moved their hearts.

Hus attracted a considerable following in his native Bohemia and in Hungary. He also attracted a number of opponents within the Church. By 1410 the divisions between him and the orthodox theologians at the University of Prague had become deep and verged on hostility. King Wenceslas of Bohemia had tried to reconcile Hus and the orthodox lecturers at Prague, but the religious authority of the pope remained a fundamental problem. Orthodox Catholics could not tolerate any challenge to the pope's position as head of the Church (even though there were three popes at the time). Hus refused to acknowledge that any man, including the pope, was in a greater position of authority than Christ himself, and asserted that a Christian soul might make an appeal to Jesus over the popes head.

Hus knew how controversial it was to use Wycliffe's writings. Pope Alexander V had excommunicated Hus in 1410, and in 1412 a council summoned by John XXIII placed him under the major excommunication. This meant that the whole of Prague would suffer an interdict unless the city officials arrested him. So he went into voluntary exile, and taken shelter in the various castles of lords who were on his side. He continued to write and preach and his sermons were carried across the Holy Roman Empire, and also into England.

Hus could not bring about a reformation of the whole Church simply by writing and preaching. But he wanted the Church to discuss its future path with respect to the individual's direct relationship with Jesus Christ. So when the King of Hungary, Sigismund, promised him a safe conduct if he would come to Constance, in southern Germany, to discuss his ideas with the council, He decided to accept.

The council of Constance was also of deep concern to Henry V as to what reform of the church would actually involve. There was the problem of imposing religious authority, especially with regard to heresy. The decisions made at Constance concerning Wycliffe, Hus and other anti-papal reformers would determine whether Henry was justified in burning such men as heretics, or whether he should tolerate them, and perhaps even listen to them. Henry had appointed a prestigious embassy to the council. Thomas Polton had already addressed the council on Henry's behalf in December but many had still not arrived.

In October 1414 Hus set out in the company of the Bohemian lords. At each city they came to Hus sent out letters saying that all who opposed his views should come to Constance to discuss them with him. He arrived at Constance on 3 November and lodged with a widow in St Paul's Street. The next day Henry Lacembok and John of Chlum went to John XXIII to announce that Hus had come willingly to Constance under the emperor's safe conduct, and to ask that the pope not allow any interference or harm to come to Hus. The pope gave his assurance that Hus would be safe.

The enemies of Hus were also there. After three and a half weeks two bishops were sent by the cardinals and demanded that he appear before them. John of Chlum was angry at this interference, contrary to the pope's promise; but Hus willingly agreed to be examined by the cardinals as to any error in his theology. So he attended the convocation at the bishop's palace.

The council had been summoned by Pope John XXIII at the emperor's request. It had two main objectives: the re-unification of the church and ecclesiastical reformation. The first objective arose from the split between the French papacy, based at Avignon, and the Roman papacy, based at

Rome. This had divided the Church since 1378. A previous attempt to heal the schism – the council of Pisa in 1409 – had resulted only in the election of a third pope, Alexander V, who had quickly died and then replaced by John XXIII, one of the worst possible candidates for the post. The three popes were – the Pisan pope, John XXIII; the Roman pope, Gregory XII; and the Avignon pope, Benedict XIII. None of them would acknowledge the others. None wanted to give up his own papal title.

On 1 January men were arriving in their hundreds. Sigismund had arrived a week earlier. The citizens of Constance marvelled at what was happening; their city was being transformed into the greatest retail centre of the Christian world. Merchants from other towns set up their stalls in courtyards and slept under makeshift shelters or huts. It was estimated that 1,400 traders had come, including shopkeepers, furriers, shoemakers and spicerers. 1,700 musicians were either present already or on their way. So were seventy-two goldsmiths, sixteen master apothecaries, and seven hundred prostitutes, who hired their own houses or who lay in stables.

The meeting at the bishop's palace was a trap. The cardinals soon departed, praising Hus's honest intentions, but leaving him in the palace, which was surrounded by armed guards. That same night Hus was moved to a cardinal's house, and after eight days he was sent to the Dominican monastery situated on an island in the Rhine, and chained up in a round tower there, 'in a murky and dark dungeon in the immediate vicinity of a latrine'.

Although John of Chlum petitioned the emperor for Hus's release, in line with the imperial safe conduct he had been granted, Hus remained in his dungeon and he became very ill because of the fumes from the latrine. The Pope ordered that he was to be moved to another cell.

In his less dangerous cell Jan Hus wrote letters to his supporters and friends in Bohemia. In writing those letters he knew that even though he had come voluntarily to Constance, he understood that he might die there.

By April 1415, Hus knew that the end was in sight. There was no hope of being found innocent.

In the same month a clergyman was making his way furtively through the streets of Constance. Jerome was a short, stout man, with a broad thick black beard. He knew the dangers of being caught. He knew that his fellow radical theologian, Jan Hus, was already in already in prison. Beneath his cloak Jerome carried a placard. It stated that Jan Hus taught and preached the truth, and that all the charges against him had been made out of enmity. He placed the placard in a prominent place and hurried away. He left Constance that same day, seeking refuge in a priest's house in the forest outside the city. Unfortunately he left his sword behind at the house in St Paul's Street where he had stayed the previous night. It was handed over to the authorities who sent out people to find the man who had come amongst them, stirring up further trouble.

As the council openly sought Wycliffe's 'condemnation' it followed that his supporters must also be condemned. For this reason Jerome of Prague now also appeared in their reckoning. He was accused of heresy and of disseminating libellous pamphlets. When news of Jerome's arrest was announced, 'many were glad, and lauds were rung', wrote Ulrich Richental in Constance. Something of the medieval sense of bloodletting as a remedy for illness seems to have taken hold of the people. The Church as a body was sick; its humours were out of balance. Thus to restore the Church to health, some blood needed to be let. Jerome and Hus would provide that blood.

On Saturday April 6, The archbishop of Riga led Hus into the cathedral for the purpose of unfrocking him. He was forbidden to speak during this ceremony. They cursed him with every holy garment they took from him, and when he stood in just gown and black coat they took a pair of scissors and obliterated his tonsure, removing most of his hair. They placed a paper mitre on his head, which bore the images of two devils and the word, *heresiarch*, shouting 'we commit your soul to the devil!'

'And I commit it to the most merciful Lord Jesus Christ, who bore a much heavier and harsher crown of thorns!' replied Hus.

They led him out of the cathedral and delivered him into the hands of the executioners. His books were being burnt nearby. Crowds had gathered to watch him go, and more now arrived. So many people were now crowding around Hus that the guards had to force them back from the bridge out of the city. Once across, Hus's executioners led him off the road that led to Gottleiben Castle and around the edge of a meadow beside the road, to the place where the stake was. Two wagon loads of straw and brushwood stood ready. People in the crowd following started shouting that he should have a confessor before he died but a mounted priest, wearing a green suit with a red silk lining, shouted back that he had been excommunicated, and deserved no confessor.

More people were flocking to the place of execution.

Ulrich Richental, who was an eyewitness, estimated that there were three thousand armed men there. He was standing near as Hus approached the stake; Richental saw him fall to his knees and scream to Christ for mercy. At the place of execution he was offered a confession on the condition that he recant. 'I am no mortal sinner!' he yelled, terrified. So they proceeded.

Hus was tied to the stake with ropes, his hands being tied behind his back. He was made to stand on a stool, and a sooty chain fastened around his neck. The executioners took brushwood and straw from the wagons and piled it around him. They scattered a little pitch over it, and lit the fire.

Hus began to sing. 'Christ thou son of the living God, have mercy on us.' As he sang the wind caught the flames and the smoke and flames began to rise into his face, and for those who saw him it seemed his lips were moving but they could hear nothing. Soon they heard not singing but the cries and screams of excruciating pain, as the fire burnt his gown and his skin. The executioners piled on more straw and brushwood. And so he died.

The paper mitre on Hus's head did not burn straightaway, according to Richental, so the executioners knocked it off into the flames with a stick. They had orders to ensure that no trace of him remained. Everything he wore on the day of his death was to be obliterated with him. And the full extent of this order became clear as the flames died down. The executioners knocked his charred flesh into the fire, and broke the bones with clubs so that they would be burned more thoroughly. As the fire died down they found his skull, dragged it out, and smashed it open with their clubs. The pieces they threw back into the flames.

The ashes were guarded. When cold enough, they were gathered up and cast into the Rhine.

On Wednesday, September 11, Jerome's nerve failed. Rather than face the terrible fate of being burnt, he chose to recant and publicly assent to his faith in the Catholic Church. To this end he had written a confession in his own hand, which he read out at a special session of the council to judge his case. However, the form of his confession was not considered explicit or full enough, so he was required to rewrite it more explicitly. The date of 23 September was assigned for him to read this revised confession, which included his rejection of the doctrines of John Wycliffe and his friend Jan Hus. On that day he would go so far as to approve of the burning of Jan Hus.

On 26 May 1416, he withdrew his recantation and his renunciation of his faith in the teachings of Wycliffe and Hus. He stood up for himself, revoked his earlier confession and boldly declared himself to be a follower of Hus. He was burnt four days later and died in great agony, for he endured the flames much longer than Hus had done, screaming terribly throughout the ordeal. His bones and ashes were broken up and dumped in the Rhine, like those of his friend.

PART 11

Franny Moyle, in her very detailed book about the life and times of Hans Holbein, 'The King's Painter,' gives us a view of Europe in the 1520's. '...Despite these endless and exhausting conflicts there had been one thing that had bound Europeans together in the early sixteenth century, and that had been their shared religion under the authority of the Pope. This ancient institution was in need of an overhaul, and yet there was hope. Erasmus was not alone in recognising the need for reform within the church. He and others saw a new way forward for European society, one where pity and kindness was valued. They had even mooted the possibility of a new kind of Christian monarch who might eschew war. There was an opportunity to cast away superstition, corruption and injustice in favour of genuine piety, self-knowledge and good governance. Perhaps there might even be a way to end war.

'However, by the early 1520's these exciting ideas had also began to sow widespread factionalism and discord. Instead of seeing an improvement in the lot of the European, Holbein and his contemporaries were witness to a new religious crisis that plunged the continent into yet deeper discord. Luther in particular had unleashed the idea of the Antichrist and a significant portion of Europe's population had consequently developed a vehement hatred of the established Papal Church, wars once fought along lines of national or regional interest were now intensified by religious ideology. What had begun as debate about the state of the church had turned into dissent and division. Protest was turning into fully fledged violence.'

'Christianity,' writes Meic Pearse, in his book 'The Great Restoration,' had begun in the Roman Empire as a dissident sectarian movement – subversive and persecuted. As the Roman intellectual Celsus sneered, it was the refuge of 'the foolish, dishonourable and stupid … slaves, women and little children.' It did not seek to convert governments but people; it did not focus on public rituals but on the attitude of the heart. One entered such a church by personal regeneration. Yet by the Middle Ages – and the effects have continued into the modern world – this church had become a monster, claiming universal authority over human society. Its infinitely numerous rules and regulations affected every part of political and social life and participation of the whole population was compulsory. Deviations from its orthodoxy (which in any case differed from the orthodoxy of the early church) was, moreover, punishable ultimately by death at the stake.

'Christianity and Judaism had thus traded places. The objects of persecution had changed too. The infant church had suffered persecution from the synagogues; medieval Christendom persecuted the Jews with a savagery that was not abated by the Reformation, and the pogroms have continued down to modern times.

'The radicals did not wish to reform Christendom, but to abandon it. They wished to restore the model of the New Testament church, complete with its sectarian pattern of operations and its minority status as an elite fellowship of the truly converted.

'The price of such all-out discipleship was clear to them from the start: persecution. But then that had been the price demanded of the early church too. In any case, these radicals were willing to pay.

'The Anabaptists were accused of rejecting civil government because they denied the right of secular authorities to govern people's consciences by enforcing one form of religion and forbidding others ... to almost all people before the late seventeenth century the idea that more than one religion in a state was consistent with social order seemed nonsensical.'

A very contentious issue was a 'believers baptism.' Infant baptism was rejected as faith was required before a person should be baptised. Luther could not agree with that position. In his preface to his commentary on Galatians he writes, 'Who cannot see here in the Anabaptists, not men possessed by demons, but demons themselves possessed by worse demons?'

Michael Sattler, a German born about 1490, became a Benedictine monk at a monastery near Freiburg. Convinced of the essential truth of the Protestant reformer's ideas, he left the cloister and got married to a woman who used to belong to a semi-monastic community which was a heinous sin in the eyes of the Roman Catholic authorities, and one which would be raised at his trial as amongst the most serious charges against him.

Converted to Anabaptism in 1525. He went to Zurich but was expelled as an undesirable alien. From there he went to Strassburg, where a number of other radicals were already beginning to gather.

The city itself had a degree of autonomy within the Holy Roman Empire. It was perhaps the most religiously tolerant city in Europe. The official situation was that Strassburg's leading clergymen, Martin Bucer and Wolfgang Capito, were slowly moving the city in the direction of reformed, rather than Lutheran, Protestantism.

Capito was disinclined to persecute dissenters, while both he and the less leniently minded Bucer were extremely impressed by the Anabaptist former prior who now confronted them.

The debate with Bucer and Capito helped Sattler himself to see the issues in a clearer light. Believer's baptism could not possibly co-exist with a state supported church; It demanded a congregation restricted to committed believers only. He began preaching this message in the Black Forest area around the town of Horb, where he was successful in planting an Anabaptist church.

Sattler was a leading figure in calling together and organizing the Schleitheim Conference of anabaptist leaders on February 24, 1527, and was the probable author of the resultant *Schelitheim Confession*, which was to be definitive of evangelical Anabaptist distinctives. It was while he was at the conference that his church was detected by the authorities, and on his return to Horb he, and his wife and some friends were arrested. He was taken to the nearby village of Binsdorf because of the protests of the Horb population at these arrests. From there he wrote a letter to what remained of his congregation; clearly anticipating his own death, warning his flock not to flee 'the surefooted and living way of Christ, namely through cross, misery, imprisonment, self-denial and finally through death.' It is not, one fears, an emphasis that would hold much appeal today, but it was certainly necessary in the circumstances.

Although the local authorities were not anxious to start a case that was certain to end in the death sentence, the imperial government based in Vienna had no such qualms, indeed, it was eager to get proceedings underway, presumably to serve as a deterrent to further radical activity. The trial was between local jurisdiction and autonomy and the powers of central and imperial government. The trial began on May 17.

Sattler found himself facing a number of charges. The first stated that he had broken the imperial mandate outlawing Lutheranism. Sattler denied the charge, pointing out that the mandate attacking Lutheranism had ordered people to follow only 'the gospel and the Word of God' which, he added, was precisely what he and his followers were doing. The second charged him with sacramentarianism, which Satler admitted; the body of Christ was at the right hand of the Father and so could not be in the bread of communion. The third charge was that he did not believe infant baptism to be necessary to salvation; again, Sattler admitted the charge, pointing out that faith was what saved a person. Accused in the fourth charge of denying the efficacy of the 'sacrament of unction' with oil, Sattler said, 'oil was good stuff since it had been made by God, but no amount of clerical or papal jiggery-pokery could improve it, for the pope has never has never made anything good'.

The fifth charge claimed that he despised 'the mother of God and the saints'. Sattler disagreed; Mary was a marvellous woman, but that did not mean she was a mediatrix between God and mankind; even she must like us await judgement, while we who live and believe are the saints'. What Sattler said was as if he trampled on the central beliefs of Catholicism. Accused of denying that Christians should take oaths, he pleaded guilty, pointing to the scriptural justification for his position. Charged with forsaking his order of monks and getting married, he pointed to the fornication in which, he said, most monks lived. Were his accusers the men whom the apostle Paul had prophesied would, in the last days, forbid marriage?

The last accusation was perhaps Sattler's most provocative remark of all. He had apparently suggested that, 'if the Turk were to come into the land, one should not resist him, and, if it were right to go to war, he would rather go to war against the Christians than the Turk'.

Already guaranteed an unpleasant execution at some time in the near future, the ex-prior decided there was no point in wasting words back and forth. 'It was wrong to resist evil with evil for you shall not kill'.

'As to me saying that if waging war were proper I would rather take the field against the so-called Christians who persecute, take captive, and kill true Christians, than against the Turks: the Turk is a genuine Turk and knows nothing of the Christian faith. He is a Turk according to the flesh. But you claim to be Christians, boast of Christ, and still persecute the faithful witnesses of Christ. Thus you are Turks according to the Spirit'.

It was not a speech calculated to tickle the ears of his audience.

He was sentenced to have his tongue cut out, to be chained to a wagon, to have his body torn seven times with red-hot tongs, and finally to be burnt at the stake. Two days later, on 20 May, the sentence was carried out. Four others were beheaded shortly after the execution. His wife, after the failure of attempts by the Countess of Zollern to persuade her to recant, was drowned eight days later in the River Neckar.

The Anabaptists were seeking to restore primitive Christianity as they understood it. One of their number, Wolfgang Brandhuber, identified the restoration of a true baptism and a true eucharist as key elements in the restoration of a true and pure church in preparation for Christ's second coming. He paid for his opinions with his life in 1529. They taught about conversion and discipleship and a willingness to accept persecution and a life as sheep amongst wolves.

A decree of the Zurich Council, March 1526:

'Whereas our Lords the Burgomaster, Council, and Great Council have for some time past earnestly endeavoured to turn the misguided and erring Anabaptists from their errors and yet several … to the injury of the public authority and the magistrates as well as to the ruin of the common welfare and of right Christian living, have proved disobedient; and several of them, men, women and girls, have been by our Lords sharply punished and put into prison: Now therefore, by the earnest commandment, edict and warning of our lords aforesaid, it is ordered that no one in our town, country or domains, whether man, woman or girl, shall baptise another; and if any hereafter shall baptise another, he will be seized by our lords and, according to the decree now set forth, will be drowned without mercy'.

PART 12

In the book about Hans Holbein, already quoted from, by Franny Moyle, she writes of Antwerp in the 1520s. 'Antwerp was also a city of secrets. It enjoyed a level of tolerance for freedom of expression and new thinking that Basel had just lost. The busy port had just become a haven underground literature; the merchant ships docking there regularly used to smuggle evangelical literature across to England, either hidden within the unbound pages of books in barrels, or slid inside bales of cloth. In the very year Holbein passed through the port, William Tyndale, an English scholar and preacher who had begun a mission to translate the Bible from the Greek and Hebrew version into English, an act at this stage punishable by death in England, had found refuge in Antwerp in the home of a sympathetic merchant Thomas Poyntz, who lived at the appropriately named English House in the city'.

Heresy had been declared to be 'treason against God' by Pope Innocent III in 1199, and was thus regarded as the worst of all crimes. Its 'vileness' was said to 'render pure even Sodom and Gomorrah', while the great medieval theologian Thomas Aquinas declared that it separated man from God more than any other sin. The Church imposed a double jeopardy on heretics. The earthly *poena senus*, the punishment of the senses, was achieved by the stake and the fire. If, like Wycliffe, the person was convicted after he was dead, the penalty was imposed on his remains. The *poena damni* proclaimed by the bishops on Wycliffe pursued his soul into the life everlasting. It damned him to absolute separation from God and to an eternity in hell.

The Church could not itself carry out a burning. To do so would defy the principle that *Eclesia non novit sanguinem*, the Church does not shed blood. Pope Lucius III had bypassed this inconvenience in 1184 by decreeing that unrepentant heretics should be handed over to the secular authorities for sentence and execution.

Oxford was known as the Vineyard of the Lord for its learning and its beauty – 'a place gladsome and fertile, suitable for a habitation of the gods' Wycliffe had written of it – but Tyndale found its teaching sterile and antiquated. Undergraduates were forbidden to speak in English – it was compulsory for them to use Latin, although French was tolerated as an alternative in some colleges. Tyndale's love of English – 'our mother tongue', he said, 'which doth correspond with scripture better than ever Latin may' – was eccentric. The English themselves largely governed, educated and prayed in Latin. Erasmus, lived for several years in England, and followed a lively social and academic life, without speaking any English.

Tyndale improved himself 'in knowledge of tongues and other liberal arts', laying the basis of his translating genius. He found the Oxford theologians, however, to be 'old barking curs ... beating the pulpit with their fists for madness'.

The great enemies in his life – Sir Thomas More, Cardinal Wolsey, and two bishops of London, Cuthbert Tunstall and John Stokesley – were between fifteen and eighteen years older than him. In 1515, while Tyndale was still at Oxford, More was on a diplomatic mission to Antwerp. There he had begun to write Utopia, his evocation of a magical island of happiness and fair-play, where reason and justice reign, but Utopia means a 'non-place', as the name of its great city, Amaurotum, comes from the Greek for 'darkly seen', and for More this ideal was an irony reflecting on the brutishness of reality.

Scores of thousands of pamphlets written by Luther came off the German presses, and they were soon flooding into England. By 1521, the English Church was so alarmed at the scale of smuggling that Wolsey presided over a grand burning of Lutheran books at St Paul's Cross in London. A few weeks later another bonfire was lit at Cambridge.

Henry VIII himself was tempted into attacking Luther – Wolsey 'furnished the court with chaplains of his own sworn disciples,' Tyndale wrote, 'to be always present, and to dispute the vanities, and to water whatsoever the cardinal had planted' – and put his name to a treatise defending Catholic orthodoxy against Lutheranism.

The English printer Richard Pynson published the king's *Asserto Septem Sacramentorum* in 1521. The actual author of this work, which won Henry the title of Defender of the Faith from the pope (the Latin abbreviation of *Fid. Def.* appears on English coins to this day), was Thomas More.

The battle lines of the coming conflict were being drawn up. More, humanist and author, but also rising lawyer and government officer – he was knighted in 1521 – appointed himself as the great lay champion of orthodoxy. Tyndale was coming to the end of his time at Cambridge. More wrote later that Tyndale at this time was known 'for a man of right good living, studious and well learned in scripture, and in divers places in England was very well liked, and did great good in preaching'. It was the only kind thing that More ever said of him.

We know that other reformers were Cambridge men, and that they were said to meet at The White Horse Inn: Hugh Latimer, Thomas Cranmer, Thomas Bilney and others whom we know Tyndale met later – Robert Barnes, Miles Coverdale and John Frith.

What is certain is that all of them, except Coverdale alone, were burnt for their beliefs; and that, at some time while he was at Cambridge, Tyndale was exposed to Luther's ideas and took his own first steps to the stake.

Tyndale knew that the Church would condemn him, but he had already been exposed to the malice of his fellow clergy in Gloucestershire, and he had survived. If the Church thought his ideas to be heresy, lay people like the Walshes had found them sympathetic (Tyndale had been employed by Sir John Walsh who was married to Anne Poyntz)

Bible-women, and Bible-reading artisans, roused a particular horror. 'Even silly little women want to pass judgement on the Bible as they might on their needle and thread.' One traditionalist wrote. A Catholic loyalist, Cochlaeus, and More, both noted the eagerness of women readers. 'Despicable women, proudly rejecting the supposed ignorance of men,' Cochlaeus wrote, were looking to the Bible rather than the Church for evidence of God's purpose; some of them 'carried it in their bosoms and learnt it by heart' and within a few months thought themselves so well versed in scripture that 'without timidity they debated not only with Catholic laymen, but also with priests and monks'.

Tyndale and his age came to the Bible, and to Christ, with a raw hunger and amazement, as if the astonishing story of the brief passage of the Son of God on earth was new to them, and as if it was only when they were released from the Latin that the words of Christ's passion struck home. In Latin, it was the priestly text of a religion whose true substance was the Church and its liturgy and tradition. Translated into a living language, devoured from cover to cover, read secretly in corners or aloud with trusted friends, its impact was wholly new; troubling, a cause of spiritual collapse and ecstasy, a divider of families, a breaker of kingdoms.

The Bible made no mention of the papacy, or of bishops or hierarchies. It was silent on the celibacy of priests. It did not state that the sacramental bread and wine was 'transubstantiated' into the body and blood of Christ at communion. It did not encourage the cult of saints and relics, from which the Church derived much income and prestige. The word 'purgatory' appeared nowhere in it; it was a twelfth- century invention. Men and women left large sums of money to chantry priests to perform 'trentals', a series of thirty intercessionary masses for their souls. Henry VII had made special efforts to avoid purgatory; the old king ordered ten thousand masses for his own soul at 6d apiece, twice the standard fee.

PART 13

Evangelicals claimed that More broke the law in his treatment of those he suspected of dealing or sympathising with Tyndale. In several cases he illegally detained them at his house in Chelsea. More created extensive gardens around his new property. A large, formal knot garden to the north led into orchards and meadows stretching towards the distant hills, where the outline of the village of Kensington could just be made out. In what would become recognised as one of the most beautiful gardens in England's Renaissance era, More's intellectual and physical worlds aligned. A menagerie of animals that included birds, a monkey, a fox, a weasel, and a ferret, plus different breeds of dog was housed there, providing not only entertainment but also a reminder of a wider animal kingdom.

He was, of course, less fond of heretics. His garden had a 'tree of truth' which More used as a whipping post. The porter's lodge in the gatehouse was fitted out with stocks, and with chains and fetters, to pinion suspects while he interrogated them.

More said that the flogging charges were the invention

of a Cambridge book dealer, Segar Nicholson, whom he arrested and kept in his house for four or five days in 1530 for selling banned books by Tyndale and others. Nicholson claimed that he had been whipped at the tree in the garden, and that cords had been wound round his head and tightened until he fainted. More denied it.

He claimed that only two heretics had been flogged at his orders. One was a boy in his service who came from a heretical family – the father had known George Joye – and who had denied the real presence of Christ in the sacrament. 'I caused a servant of mine to stripe like a child before mine household,' More wrote, 'for amendment of himself and example of such other.' The other was a local lunatic, 'which after he had fallen into the frantic heresies, fell soon after into plain open frenzy beside,' More wrote mockingly; the man would creep up behind a woman in church, and lift up her skirts and throw them over her head. He was pointed out to More as he passed the Chelsea house. The chancellor had him seized, tied to the garden tree and publicly flogged. 'They striped him with rods until he waxed weary and somewhat longer,' More wrote with evident self-satisfaction.

He agreed that he had often sentenced mem to be flogged for robbery, murder, or 'sacrilege in church, with carrying away the pyx with the blessed sacrament, or villainously casting it out'. But he denied that he had commanded any other heretics to be flogged, 'notwithstanding also that heretics be yet much worse than all they'.

There had been no burnings in England for eight years. More soon put a stop to that. He did not quite condemn his predecessors – 'I will not say that the judges did wrong' – but he made it clear that he thought them lax. The heretic had been mollycoddled, allowed to escape through recantation and faggot-carrying, and in this the bishops and church officers were 'almost more than lawful, in that they admitted him to such an abjuration as they did, and that they did not rather leave him to the secular arm'. He concluded that 'in the condemnation of heretics, the clergy might lawfully do much more sharply than they do'.

A priest named Thomas Hitton was the first to suffer from More's new 'sharpness'. He was seized near Gravesend in January 1530 as he was making his way to the coast to take a ship for Antwerp. Hitton had fled to join Tyndale and the English exiles in the Low Countries after becoming a convinced evangelical. He returned to England on a brief visit to contact supporters of Tyndale and to arrange for the distribution of smuggled books.

Hitton was walking through fields by the coast, his mission completed, when he was stopped by a posse of men looking for a thief who had stolen some linen that was drying on a hedge. They searched him. He had no linen, but hidden pockets were found in his coat that held letters 'unto the evangelycall heretykes beyonde the see'. Unfortunately for Hitton, the new chancellor's strictures on heretics were fresh in people's minds. The men handed Hitton over to the archbishop of Canterbury's officers.

At his interrogation before the archbishop. Hitton refused to recant and remained true to his new beliefs. 'The mass he sayed sholde never be sayed'. it was recorded of his answers. 'Purgatory he denied ... No man hath ant fre wyll after he hath ons synned ... all the images of Cryste and his sayntes sholde bde thrown out of the chyrche'.

Sentence was swiftly passed and executed: Thomas

Hitton was burnt alive at Maidstone on 23 February 1530. He was the first of the Reformation martyrs. The English exiles in Antwerp were shocked. They had a new calendar printed with 23 February marked as the 'day of St Thomas'.

More had written, 'God hath taught his church without writing'. How had God managed this feat? The New Testament, as Tyndale had written on his title page, was 'written, and caused to be written, by them which heard it, it being the word of God. Who had heard these later things that God had taught? How had they heard? Why had they not written them down?

Tyndale knew well enough what Catholic apologists like More actually meant. For fourteen hundred years, the Church had been the guardian of the Christian spirit. It had distilled the thoughts of the great men of the past, the ancient Fathers and figures like Augustine, Bernard, Gregory and Aquinas, into a tradition so laboriously acquired. Compared to all the Church had made and accomplished, the Bible was no more than a relic of dusty parchment. To More, the Christian religion was so identified with the Church that it seemed natural that God should whisper truths into its collective ear. The Church had acquired God's word through osmosis, as it were, by a gradual and unwritten absorption over the centuries.

At times, More's passion for heretic burning runs almost out of control! 'There should have more burned by a great many than there have been within this seven-year last past'. he wrote. More looked forward to the fires, and fantasised on the punishments he would inflict on Tyndale and Luther. 'If the zele of god were amonge men that should be,' he wrote, 'such rayling rybalds that so mokke with holy scripture, shold at every exposycyon have an hote iren thruste thorow theyr blasphemouse tonges'.

'Tyndale's bokes,' More wrote, 'and theyr owne malyce maketh them heretykes. And for heretykes as they be, the clergy dothe burne them, and after the fyre of Smythfelde, hell doth receyue them, where the wretches burne foreuer'.

The urge to martyrdom was as old as the faith itself. To die in imitation of Christ was the noblest of all fates in itself, and it had long been observed that it also served to spread the dead man's belief among the living. Pliny the Younger, adopted son of the great natural historian and the Roman governor of Bithynia, had noted in about AD 112 that persecuting Christians for their 'depraved and extravagant superstition' was fine in theory, but in practice produced 'the usual result of spreading the crime'.

Tertullian, one of the Fathers of the Church, confirmed this a century later. 'The blood of martyrs,' he said, 'is the seed of the Church'.

Thomas Bilney, one of the Cambridge scholars, who had escaped Wolsey in 1527, and who had abjured in front of Tunstall in 1529, did not survive the new Lord Chancellor. Bilney, a short man, was seized in March 1531 and brought in front of Bishop Nix of Norwich.

He was convicted of heresy and 'relaxed' to the secular power. Foxe (John Foxe's Book of Martyrs) says that More sent down the writ to burn him. Bilney practised for his martyrdom in his cell by burning his fingers in a candle, constantly repeating Isaiah's words: 'When you walkest through the fire, thou shalt not be burnt'. It was nearly harvest time, and he compared himself to the straw in the fields. 'Howsoever the stubble of this my body shall be wasted' by the fire, he told himself, 'yet my soul and spirit shall be purged there by: a pain for a time, whereupon notwithstanding followeth joy unspeakable'.

While he was waiting to be bound to the stake, in the Lollard's sandpit at Norwich, on 19 August 1531, Bilney repeated the creed as proof that he died as a true Christian, and offered up a prayer; 'Enter not into judgement with thy servant, O Lord, for in thy sight no living flesh can be justified'. The day, to his misfortune, was windy enough to damage the harvest crops. The executioner first set his torch to the reeds round the stake. These made a great flame which disfigured Bilney's face. He held up his hands and cried 'Jesus!' and 'Credo!' The flame was 'blown away from him several times, the wind being very high', and 'for a little pause, he stood without flame, the fire departing and recoursing'. It was many minutes before the wood caught solidly afire, and, so More wrote with satisfaction, 'God, of hys endless mercy brought hys body to deth'.

More's abiding passion remained the taking of Tyndale and the destruction of his friends, such as Richard Bayfield, John Tewkesbury and James Bainham, a barrister of Middle Temple who was a popular man whose execution angered Londoners. In his interrogation in front of More and Stokesley he was asked if a person should honour and pray to dead saints. 'Jesus Christ the just is the propitiation for our sins,' he replied, 'and not only for our sins, but for the sins of the whole world.' To pray to saints thus had no purpose. What, then, did St Paul mean when he wrote: 'Let all the saints of God pray for us'? Paul, Bainham said, meant living saints, not the dead, because 'they which be dead cannot pray for him'.

Was it necessary for his salvation that a man confess his sins to a priest? 'Sins are to be forgiven of God,' Bainham replied, 'and a man need not go to any confession.'

What did he mean by saying that the truth of holy scripture had been hidden for eight hundred years until now? 'I mean no other wise,' he said, 'but that the truth was never, these eight hundred years past, so plainly and expressly declared unto the people, as it hath been within these six years.'

What has happened in the last six years to make him say this? 'The New Testament now translated into English, doth preach and teach the word of God,' he said, 'and before that time men did not preach but only that folks should believe as the church did believe, and then if the church erred, men should err too.'

This claim that the Church had purloined the Bible for its own false purposes was the very heart of the matter. Bainham added a comment that sealed his fate. 'Howbeit the church of Christ cannot err,' he said, 'and there are two churches. That is, the church of Christ militant, and the church of Antichrist, and that this church of Antichrist may and doth err, but the church of Christ doth not.'

Bainham was now asked if he knew of anyone who had lived in the true faith of Christ since the apostles. 'I knew Bayfield,' he said of More's recent victim. 'He died in the true faith of Christ.'

What did he think of purgatory? 'If any such thing as purgatory after this like had been moved to St Paul,' came the answer, 'he would have condemned it for heresy.'

And what of vows on holy orders? On the celibacy of priests? 'Vows of chastity, and all godliness, is given of God by his abundant grace, which no man himself can keep, but it must be given him of God,' he replied. If a monk, friar or nun could not keep their vow of celibacy, 'they may go forth and marry … for there are no other vows, than the vow of baptism'.

Were the bread and wine of the sacraments not the body and blood of Christ? The king was at his most sensitive on this point. Henry remained proud of his treatise defending the traditional view of the sacraments; he flew into a rage when evangelicals meddled with it, as Bainham did now. 'The bread is not Jesus Christ, for Christ's body is not chewed with teeth, therefore it is but bread.'

He confessed that he had a copy of Tyndale's New Testament, but denied that he had offended God by keeping it and using it. He added that 'the New Testament in English was utterly good', and added that he did not know that Tyndale was a 'naughty fellow'.

Bainham could not be saved in this world, but More and Stokesley felt obliged to purge his soul before they had him burnt. He was taken first to the bishop's coal cellar at Fulham Palace, a place where many episcopal prisoners were kept. He was locked in irons, put in the stocks and left to reflect on his fate for several chilly March days. When this failed to produce any remorse, he was taken back to Sir Thomas More's house at Chelsea. Here, he was chained to a post for two nights, and whipped, before being returned to Fulham to be 'cruelly handled the space of a week'. After a further fortnight of whippings in the Tower, Bainham remained unredeemed, and charity was deemed to have run its course.

Bainham was delivered to Sir Richard Gresham, the

sheriff, who had him carried by his officers to a cell in Newgate. He was burnt on the last day of April 1532.

There were many horsemen about the stake at Smithfield, indicating a well-bred audience. Bainham embraced the stake, and then stood on the pitch barrel, with a chain about his waist held by sergeants of the guard. 'I come hither, good people', he said to the crowd, 'accused and condemned for a heretic, Sir Thomas More being my accuser and judge.' He then spoke of the beliefs for which he was to die. Foxe claims that he ticked off all the main evangelical articles. 'First, I say it is lawful for every man and woman, to have God's book in their mother tongue. Second, that the bishop of Rome is Antichrist ... there is no purgatory ...' At this, the town clerk, Master Pave, said, 'Thou liest, thou heretic! Thou deniest the blessed sacrament of the altar,' Bainham retorted that he did not deny the sacrament of Christ's body and blood, but only 'your idolatry to the bread, and that Christ God and man should dwell in a piece of bread ...' at that, Pave ordered: 'Set fire to him and burn him.'

As the train of gunpowder came towards him, Bainham lifted up his eyes and hands to heaven, and said to Pave: God forgive thee, and show thee more mercy than thou showest to me. The Lord forgive Sir Thomas More! And pray for me, all good people ...'

With that, the fire 'took his bowels and his head'.

The following week, Pave bought ropes, climbed into a high garret in his house and tried to hang himself.

Tyndale's friends and sympathisers could be burnt but the man himself continued just beyond More's reach. In the autumn of 1531, King Henry had asked the imperial authorities for his extradition to England on the grounds that he was living in subterfuge in the imperial dominions, from where he was sending seditious books to England.

The appeal fell on deaf ears for Charles V had no reason to grant Henry favours.

In the afternoon of 16 May 1532 More put the Great Seal into a white leather bag and delivered it to the king in the garden at York Place. 'Chancellor More is no more,' a wag wrote. A few days later, Henry replaced him with another lawyer, Sir Thomas Audley. More retired from active politics, passing his time in Chelsea.

He remained as busy as ever in the campaign against heresy. He had no intention of giving up the struggle against 'these newfangled sects',

Heretics, he said in a letter to Erasmus, 'have a passion for wickedness,' and pledged that 'all my efforts are directed towards the protection of those men who do not deliberately desert the truth, but are seduced by the argument of clever fellows'.

Ten men had been burnt in England since More had first become Chancellor. Tyndale knew three of them well, and may have met two more. Next to the stake went his closest and dearest friend, John Frith, a young scholar who was well respected by all who knew him. In his pursuit of Frith, More revealed all the fieldcraft – the use of double agents, political intuition and intricate manipulation of rulers and senior officials, the sowing of bribes, flattery, and inflexible and murderous intent – that he brought to bear on Tyndale.

Frith wrote his *Disputaacyon of Purgatorye*, a treatise in three books in which he argued against More and Fisher that purgatory was a recent invention of the Church that had no foundation in scripture. Cromwell urged Stephen Vaughan, a king's agent and a commercial consul in the Low Countries, to try to win over Frith. The king's instruction was that if he returned to England and if he was to 'forsake, leave and withdraw his affection from Tyndale then he will win merit from God, and thanks from the king'.

Frith did return to England, but a year later, in July 1532, and without the protection of a safe-conduct from the king. He went to Reading where he was arrested and put into the stocks as a vagrant. He refused to give his name or explain what business had brought him to the town. He asked an onlooker to bring a Reading schoolmaster to come to him so that he could prove that he was not a beggar. Leonard Cox arrived and recognised a fellow Etonian who could recite Homer's *Iliad* in the original Greek. Cox reported this to the town's governors and Frith was released.

Frith was in grave peril as he made his way through London and on to Essex to take a ship back to Antwerp. A reward was put on his head and the roads close to the coast were watched.

Like Hitton before him Frith was taken in October 1532 by the sea at Milton Shore near Southend. Cromwell arranged for Frith to be kept in loose detention, unshackled, in the Tower of London.

There was still every chance that Frith would remain safe. Cromwell wished him well. The king was impressed by reports of his learning and charming demeanour; the duke of Norfolk thought there was 'no fitter or better qualified man to send abroad on an embassy to a great prince'.

Frith was treated with great favour at the Tower and was released over Christmas and lodged by Stephen Gardiner, the bishop of Winchester, at his palace in Southwark, he had been Frith's tutor at Cambridge.

Frith wrote and received letters, from Tyndale among others. One of his letters led to his undoing. Frith was asked by a friend to write done his views on the Lord's Supper, something that Tyndale had advised him to steer clear of. We do not know who the 'friend' was but he may have been employed by More, as he received the letter that Frith had written.

Even though More was out of office, he was keeping his network of informants well oiled.

Archbishop Cranmer sent one of his gentlemen, and a Welsh porter, to bring Frith from the Tower to his palace in Croydon to be examined. Cranmer's gentleman advised Frith to be prudent and non-controversial for not only his sake but also for his wife and children across the sea. While Cranmer and Cromwell wished him well, he had enemies who wanted him burnt.

As they continued their journey they passed the woods of Brixton. Cranmer's man suggested that Frith make off into the woods and travel east to his native Kent, while he and the porter would first search the woods to the west towards Wandsworth before raising the alarm, but Frith refused the offer. Before he was taken on the Essex shore, he said, he had tried everything to escape; but now that he was face to face with his enemies, he felt he had to testify to his faith and remain true to God.

He was held overnight in the porter's lodge at Croydon. He held resolutely to his belief that the sacramental bread and wine were no more than symbols of Christ's Body and Blood.

Cranmer saw him in private three times to ask him to 'leave his imagination', but he would not. On 17 June 1533, Cranmer wrote that: 'We had to leave him to his ordinary.' That meant that he was given over to the mercies of Stokesley, the bishop in whose diocese he had been taken. On 20 June, Frith appeared in front of Stokesley, Gardiner and Langland in St Paul's Cathedral. He again refused to abjure. 'The cause why I die is this,' he said, 'for I cannot agree ... that we should believe under pain of damnation, the substance of the bread and wine to be changed into the body and blood of our Saviour.' He signed his heretical answers in his own hand: 'I, Frith, thus do think, and as I think, so have I said, written, taught, and affirmed, and in my books have published.' Stokesley declared him guilty for having denied that the doctrines of purgatory and transubstantiation were necessary articles of faith. He was relaxed to the secular power for execution on 23 June.

From Antwerp, Tyndale sent a last letter to his friend urging strength in facing the fire. 'Dearly beloved,' he wrote, 'fear not men that threat, nor trust men that speak fair: but trust him that is true of promise, and able to make his word good. Your cause is Christ's gospel, a light that must be fed with the blood of faith. The lamp must be dressed and snuffed daily, and that oil poured in every evening and morning, that the light go not out ... If when we be buffeted for well-doing, we suffer patiently and endure, that is thankful with God; for to that end we are called. For Christ also suffered for us, leaving us an example that we should follow his steps, who did no sin. Hereby have we perceived love that he laid down his life for us: therefore we ought to be able to lay down our lives for the brethren ...

Let not your body faint. If the pain be above your strength, remember: 'Whatsoever ye shall ask in my name, I will give it you.' And pray to your Father in that name, and he will ease your pain, or shorten it … Amen.'

In a grim postscript, Tyndale gave details of the agony of other Bible-men: 'Two have suffered in Antwerp unto the great glory of the gospel: four at Lille in Flanders: and at Liege one at the least hath suffered; all that same day. At Rouen in France they persecute; and at Paris are five doctors taken for the gospel. See, you are not alone.'

Tyndale closed his letter, 'your wife is well content with the will of God, and would not, for her sake, have the glory of God hindered.'

The prisoner was held in Newgate prison, his neck bound to a post by an iron collar. On 4 July 1533, he was taken to Smithfield with Andrew Hewitt, a young tailor's apprentice who had also been betrayed to More by the same agent that had betrayed Frith. The rector who addressed the crowd forbade them to pray for the prisoners, no more than they would for a dog. At this, Frith smiled and asked God to forgive the rector. Foxe says that the wind blow the flames away from Frith, so that his dying was prolonged, but he showed no sign of pain.

To the burning of his dearest friend in England, Tyndale now had to add a sharp increase in the danger in Antwerp. Catholic loyalists were angry and militant at the headway that reform was making in the city.

They sent a long and detailed letter to the chancellor of Brabant in 1533, giving details of local Lutherans and other heretics. They insisted that the chancellor take action, 'We have given you material enough … Do as they have done in Spain. Purge the town. Strengthen the laws; make half-yearly searches after heretics.'

A priest named in the letter was arrested, taken to the state prison at Vilvoorde Castle, and burnt at Brussels the following year. Two laymen, who had attended a church declared to be a nest of heresy by the informers, were beheaded in Antwerp. The printer Adriaen van Berghen was interrogated in 1533 but managed to extricate himself. Three years later, he was condemned for selling Letheren books and was forced to make his penitential pilgrimage to Cyprus; returning to his old ways, he was later arrested at Delft and executed. Another Antwerp printer, Jacob van Liesvelt, was also later beheaded for printing Bibles in Flemish.

Tyndale had recently turned forty. He had every reason to look forward to completing his life's work, in the comfortable and sympathetic surroundings of the English House in Antwerp. Or perhaps in England. The two men most in the ascendancy, Cromwell and Cranmer, were favourable to reform. An English Bible was within a whisker of gaining official approval. No royal command was issued, but Miles Coverdale began to integrate Tyndale's existing translations into a complete Bible, dedicated to Henry VIII. Coverdale was a Cambridge reformer and renegade Augustinian friar who had fled abroad in 1528; Foxe says he joined Tyndale in Hamberg in 1529, staying with him in the house of the widow Margaret von Emerson, and helped him in the translating of the whole five books of Moses. Coverdale based his work on Tyndale where he could.

Tyndale's great enemy was still writing furiously from Chelsea warning of the 'corrupt cankar' of heretics – but

More was himself now in peril as the king's anger with papal loyalists grew apace.

More, who was locked in the Tower for refusing to swear the Oath of Succession, now faced the traitor's agony of hanging, drawing and quartering. He feared the distress he would have to go through and discovered his fear of pain and the thought of such a death was more than he, as a faithful Christian man, could bear.

As the summer and autumn of 1534 passed into winter, More remained in the Tower. His legal situation deteriorated further after parliament passed the Act of Supremacy in November. This confirmed the king to be 'the only supreme head in earth of the Church of England, called *Anglicana Ecclesia*'.

At the close of 1534, Thomas More was thinking of William Tyndale, and what he wished to happen to him.

On 21 May 1535, the day of his betrayal, Tyndale had sixteen months more to live. More had a little over six weeks.

PART 14

Tyndale was relaxed enough by now to enjoy a social life among the merchants, and he was often invited to dinner and supper with them. He met Harry Phillips – who was in his middle twenties and came from a good family, he was also well schooled – and took a shine to him.

If Harry Phillips had ever been what he appeared to be – friendly, honest, scholarly and true – he ceased to be so after he left Oxford. He robbed his father of a sum of money entrusted to him to settle an obligation, and thereafter lived off his wits. Having squandered the money, he wrote to his mother 'piteously begging' her to intercede with his father on his behalf. He said that he had 'chanced to fall into play' while he was in London to deliver his father's money to a Mr Medlee. He had lost £3 or £4 gambling and, fearing his father's wrath, had not dared come home. Later he also lost his 'spending money', and 'by fortune he was driven he whist not whither'.

At some stage late in 1534, Harry Phillips came into a considerable amount of money, some of which he had used to enrol in the university of Louvain on 14 December 1534. That university was strictly and energetically Catholic. Had Tyndale suspected that his young friend had connections with Louvain, he would have dropped him at once.

But Tyndale, so worldly in his writing, and so artless with men, was easy prey. It is sad that he should have treated Harry Phillips with the same honest affection as he had John Frith.

After spending three or four days in Antwerp, Phillips went to the imperial court at Brussels, where he arranged that the procurer general, the imperial attorney and other government officers should go to Antwerp to seize Tyndale. This, so Foxe surmised, was 'not done with small charges or expenses, from whomsoever it came'. A resident of the English House was a sensitive person to arrest, given the importance of English trade, and it is likely that Phillips had to grease some important palms.

The arrest could only be done outside of the house. On 21 May Phillips told the wife of Poyntz, who was in charge of the House, that he wanted to eat with Tyndale and she replied that he was working in his study. Phillips left to arrange where the officers were to be positioned and returned at midday. He went to Tyndale's study and asked him to lend him 40 shillings, saying that he had lost his purse in the street that morning. It was easy to get money from Tyndale, so Foxe wrote, 'for in the wily subtleties of this world he was simple and inexpert'. At dinnertime – they ate early in those days, well before noon – the two men left the house, which was set back from the lane by a long and narrow entry that would not take the two of them abreast. Tyndale therefore gestured for Phillips to go ahead. With a great show of courtesy, Phillips insisted that the older man lead. As they walked, Phillips, who was a head taller than Tyndale, pointed down at him to identify him to the waiting officers.

The arrest was quiet and easy. Tyndale was taken to the procurer general, who gave him dinner: a distinguished scholar was not a run-of-the-mill criminal. From there he was taken to the castle of Vilvoorde, an eighteen-mile trip from Antwerp.

The last surviving words that Tyndale wrote tell us of his suffering from the cold and damp, and from the darkness. The letter is in Latin. It is not dated, but it was almost certainly written five or six months after his arrest, in the autumn of 1535.

In the letter he asks, 'by the Lord Jesus, that if I am to remain here through the winter, you will request the commissary to have the kindness to send me, from the goods of mine which he has, a warmer cap; for I suffer greatly from cold in the head, and am afflicted by a perpetual catarrh, which is much increased in this cell; a warmer coat also, for this that I have is very thin; a piece of cloth too to patch my leggings. My overcoat is worn out; my shirts are also worn out. He has a woollen shirt, If he will be good enough to send it. I have also with him leggings of thicker cloth to put on above; he also has warmer nightcaps. And I ask to be allowed to have a lamp in the evening; it is indeed wearisome sitting alone in the dark. But most of all I beg and beseech your clemency to be urgent with the commissary, that he will kindly permit me to have the Hebrew bible, Hebrew grammar, and Hebrew dictionary, that I may pass the time in that study. In return may you obtain what you most desire, so only that it be for the salvation of your soul. But if any other decision has been taken concerning me, to be carried out before winter, I will be patient, abiding the will of God, to the glory of the grace of my Lord Jesus Christ; whose spirit (I pray) may ever direct your heart.

Amen. W Tindalus.'

There was no rush to burn him. He had time to convert his keeper and his keeper's daughter, or so Foxe claims; others among the castle staff, impressed by his fortitude and sincerity, said to one another that if Tyndale 'were not a good Christian man, they could not tell whom they might take to be one'. Even Pierre Dufief, the prosecutor, agreed that his prisoner was a learned, pious and fine man.

Dufief was the main member of the commission, and the archives show that he was paid the handsome sum of £128 for his services. He had a reputation for venality as well as cruelty; he benefited from the sale of goods confiscated from his prisoners, and extortion and embezzlement seems to lie behind his eventual removal from office. He was joined by three theologians, Ruard Tapper, Jacobus Latomus and Jan Doye. It was their task to prove that Tyndale's beliefs amounted to heresy.

Tyndale's writings were thick with self-incriminating evidence. He wrote that faith alone justifies, and that salvation flows from grace and forgiveness of sins offered in the gospel. And not from good works … he held that church rulings based on human traditions cannot bind the conscience; he proclaimed the inefficacy of prayers to the saints, pilgrimage, and confession to priests.

Each of these was proof of heresy. It is doubtful whether a full confession and abjuration would have saved him.

The nub of the case, and its passion, lay in Tyndale's attachment to the Christ he had rediscovered in the gospel, and in his certainty that salvation lay in faith and in the love that God manifests through the Son. Latomus rightly identified this conviction as bible-based. 'If, as you write, you desire to be instructed,' he remarked to Tyndale, 'be careful not to regard the sacred text as a storehouse of arguments for your part.' But that, of course, was precisely what Tyndale did believe; for him, the Bible was the sole storehouse of divine truth. Latomus urged him to think again. 'Consider to what absurdity you are come to by leaving the well-trodden paths and the teachings of the Fathers.'

Tyndale was found guilty of heresy in the first days of August 1536. He was told that he was to be degraded from the priesthood and relaxed to the secular power for sentence. The process was unchanged from the days of John Hus. The three bishops – the suffragan was from Cambrai – were seated on a high wooden platform. Tyndale was led to it, in the vestments of a priest about to celebrate mass, and made to kneel in front of the bishops. His hands were scraped with the blade of a knife, symbolically removing the oil with which he had been anointed at his consecration. The sacraments were placed in his hands and taken away. As the cup was removed from him, the bishops intoned a solemn curse: 'O cursed Judas, because you have abandoned the counsel of peace and have counselled with the Jews, we take away from you this cup of redemption.' Other curses were pronounced as his stole and chasuble were stripped from him, one by one, and he was reclothed as a layman.

At the end, the bishops said the final curse: 'We commit your soul to the devil.' Having deprived him of all ecclesiastical rights, the bishops then ensured that the Church would not be stained with Tyndale's blood by proclaiming: 'We turn him over to the secular court.' Ritual demanded that Dufief acknowledge this by saying: 'I am the one who wields the temporal sword.' Tyndale was now doubly condemned. The *poena sensus* was to be achieved by his strangulation and burning; this was to be followed by the *poena damni*, confirming his absolute separation from God in the eternity of hell.

He was executed early in October 1536. A stout stake or beam was set up in a public place. Iron chains were fastened to the top of the stake, and a noose of rope passed through it at neck hight. Kindling and faggots were piled up in a pyramid around the stake. Tyndale, after refusing a final opportunity to recant, was bound to the stake, by his feet, and by the iron chains around his calves and chest. The noose was placed round his neck. The executioner, standing immediately behind the stake, tightened the noose at Dufief's signal. It had not been shown that Tyndale was a relapsed heretic, and he qualified for the mercy of being strangled in the moments before the fire was lit.

It appears that the executioner bungled his work and that Tyndale was still alive as the flames engulfed him. The executioner added fuel to the fire until the body was utterly consumed. The ashes were then disposed of so that no trace of the heretic remained to defile the earth.

Any writings found in his cell may have been burnt on the day of his execution, as had happened to John Hus.

On the 28 July 1540 the French ambassador, Charles de Marillac, sent news to France. 'Mr Thomas Cromwell, heretofore condemned by Parliament, this morning was beheaded in the usual place for such executions. Grace was made to him upon the method of his death, for his condemnation was to be a more painful and ignominious penalty.'

Jessie Childs, in her book, 'Henry VIII'S Last Victim' writes, 'Writing from the Tower with a 'heavy heart and trembling hand', Cromwell protested his innocence and begged the king for 'mercy, mercy, mercy'. He did not even get a trial. Condemned by an act of attainder, the method of persecution that he himself had so favoured.'

Marillac wrote with horror about the continuing slaughter of those who chose to disagree with the English king. Two days after Cromwell was beheaded, three doctors were 'hanged as traitors for speaking in favour of the Pope', while another three were burned as heretics for speaking against the Pope. The country was in complete confusion, Marillac relayed, not understanding quite what the English church stood for, and where 'what is commanded is so often altered that it is difficult to understand what it is'.

PART 15

Six years later it was clear that the king's life was drawing to a close. With England's political and religious future uncertain, the conservatives intensified their efforts to smash the evangelical networks. Prominent evangelical preachers Edward Crome and Nicholas Shaxton were arrested for preaching against the teaching of transubstantiation, but both recanted when threatened with burning. Others refused to buckle. Anne Askew, a woman in her early twenties, daughter of Sir William Askew, was sentenced to death for denying the doctrine of the mass. When bishop Shaxton visited her prison cell and urged her to follow his example by recanting, she likened him to Judas Iscariot. Due to Askew's close connections with ladies in the royal court, her captors tortured her in the hope that she would divulge the names of fellow evangelicals close to the king. She was stretched on the rack in the Tower of London, remarkable treatment for a woman with noble connections and a scandal when the news broke. The lieutenant of the Tower refused to continue the torture, so Sir Thomas Wriothesley (the Lord Chancellor) and Sir Richard Rich racked her with their own hands until she was almost dead. Askew was sent to Smithfield for burning on 16 July 1546, carried there in a chair because she could no longer walk. Three men were also executed with her.

PART 16

Shortly after noon on a cold and rainy late October day in 1553, a procession began at the town hall of Geneva, in western Switzerland. On the border with France. At its head were the local dignitaries – magistrates in their robes and hats, members of the town council, clergymen in their gowns, and the chief of police. Immediately behind them rode a wave of officers on horseback and a guard of mounted archers. Next came the citizens of the city, first the well-to-do burghers, then the tradespeople and artisans, and finally, a mob of the city's lower classes. Their destination was a hillside at Champel, about a mile outside the city's walls.

In the midst of these fair-skinned Swiss, one man stood out, a prisoner. He was in his forties, dark, almost Moorish, dirty and weak, with a long unkept beard and ragged clothing. He was surrounded by a crowd of pastors exhorting to confess his sins. An aging churchman, Guillaume Farel, walked next to him, whispering in his ear. The prisoner prayed silently in reply.

The prisoner's shabby appearance belied his status as one

of Europe's leading physicians and preeminent thinkers. His name was Michael Servetus, and his crime was publishing a book that redefined Christianity, although this book contained a great scientific discovery – one which a century later would propel medicine into the modern age – on that October afternoon in 1553, no one in Geneva knew or cared.

Michael Servetus had risked his life and position to publish his book, *Christianismi Restitutio* (*The Restoration of Christianity*). After running afoul of the Inquisition with an earlier version twenty years before. He changed his name to Michel de Villeneuve but he was unwilling to live out his life without being true to his beliefs. He was arrested in Vienne and put on trial. Despite the evidence against him, he brazenly denied that he was the same man as Servetus. 'Villeneuve' asserted that he was a medical doctor rather than a theologian, and that he would happily submit himself to the teaching of the catholic church. Nevertheless only two days into the trial he fled, escaping from prison by jumping over a wall. *In absentia*, Servetus was found guilty of heresy and sedition, and sentenced to death. Since he was on the run, his effigy was executed instead – it was hanged and then burned at the stake, along with five bales of blank paper representing his books.

Servetus planned to seek refuge at Naples and continue his medical practice, but on his way through Switzerland he foolishly chose to stop in Geneva.

His book proposed that the church needed to return to its original purity unencumbered by the accretions of the last fifteen centuries. In particular, he argued that the doctrine of the Trinity could not be found in the Bible and mocked the concept as the Christian equivalent of Cerberus, the three-headed dog of Greco-Roman mythology who guarded the gates of hell.

From Vienne, Servetus began a lengthy correspondence with Calvin and sent him a copy of his manuscript, but the reformer rejected these ideas as 'wild imaginings', When the Spaniard (he was born Miguel Serveto) proposed a visit to Geneva in 1547, Calvin told Farel: 'I am unwilling to guarantee his safety, for if he does come and my authority counts for anything, I will never let him get away alive.'

There he was recognised and arrested on Sunday 13 August 1553. Having escaped the clutches of his catholic enemies, he had now run straight into the hands of his evangelical ones. The case was prosecuted by the city council, not by the consistory (the normal means of ecclesiastical discipline), although Calvin was involved as a witness and their theological clashes in court were often heated. Meanwhile Calvin wrote to the pastors at Frankfurt, where the *Restitutio* was likely to be sold at the local book fair, that it contained 'nothing but a farrago of errors … a compendium of the impious ravings of all ages. There is no sort of impiety which this monster has not raked up, as if from the infernal regions.' He exhorted the pastors that it was their duty to destroy every copy.

On October 26, the Little Council met. Ami Perrin, known as a 'Libertine', for his opposition to Calvin, moved that the trial be transferred to the Council of Two Hundred. When this was voted down, Servetus was condemned without dissent: 'We condemn you, Michael Servetus, to be bound and taken to Champel and there attached to a stake and burned with your book to ashes.' Calvin wrote, 'We tried to change the mode of his death, but in vain.'

According to Calvin, Servetus received the news of his sentence with disbelief and frantic self-pity, moaning and crying out for mercy. He begged that he could speak with Calvin which was granted.

During the meeting, Calvin held out the possibility that if Servetus were to publicly renounce his views, he might die more quickly and mercifully. Servetus was himself worried that in a moment of extreme pain, he would recant and lose his soul. He begged Calvin to be allowed to die by the sword. Calvin refused and wrote: '... I reminded him gently how I had risked my life more than sixteen years ago to gain him for our Saviour. If he would return to reason I would faithfully do my best to reconcile him to all good servants of God ... I told him that I would pass over everything which concerned me personally. He should rather ask the pardon of God whom he had so basely blasphemed in his attempt to efface the three persons in one essence ... But when I saw that all this did no good I ... withdrew from the heretic who was self-condemned.'

The Council wasted no time. The next day, shortly after midday, October 27, 1553, he was lead to the stake. Every step of the way Farel walked next to him. Servetus was seated at the stake and an iron chain wrapped around his body, a crown of twigs and sulphur was placed on his head, and sticks of green wood – intended to burn more slowly and thus prolong his suffering – were lit. A copy of his book burned beneath his feet. Another account says that the book was lashed to his arm. His last recorded words were, 'Jesus, son of God eternal, have mercy on me!' As

Farel observed, even in his dying moments the heretic had obstinately refused to acknowledge Jesus as '*eternal* son of God'. It took Servetus thirty minutes to die. John Calvin stayed home.

One contemporary, the French theologian Sebastian Castellio, found the whole episode deeply shameful. For Castellio, the execution was an unforgivable act of tyranny. He began to wonder if the very notion of persecuting heretics was not a betrayal of the entire Christian cause. Just what were heretics, Castellio asked: simply 'those with whom we disagree.' And while you might detest the people with whom you quarrelled, it really wasn't appropriate to torture and kill them. Force and violence had no role to play in the arena of religious belief because the truth could not be hammered into people's minds. Persuasion was endlessly more efficient than coercion.

Castellio asked his Christ a rhetorical question. 'I beg you in the name of your Father, do you now command that those who do not understand your precepts be drowned in water, cut with lashes to the entrails, dismembered by the sword, or burned at a slow fire?' Did Christ approve of these things being done in his name? are they your vicars who make these sacrifices?' Of course not. 'O blasphemous and shameful audacity of men, who dare to attribute to Christ that which they do by the command and the instigation of Satan.'

Castellio looked for an emphasis upon Christian morality rather than doctrinal correctness, and maintained: 'It would be better to let a hundred, even a thousand heretics live than put a decent man to death under pretence of heresy.' Critics of Castellio said that 'he advises everyone to believe whatever he wants, opening the door by this means to all heresies and false doctrines'. Calvin described Castellio's teaching as 'malignant, unmanageable and pernicious'. He defended the burning of Servetus as perfectly lawful in his 1554 treatise on the doctrine of the Trinity, and in his final edition of the *Institutes* he continued to attack this executed heretic as a 'foul dog'.

In the July 2009 edition of Now, a Christian newspaper, there is a full- page article celebrating the birth of John Calvin in 1509. The article begins with 'The theologian of the Holy Spirit' is how B.B. Warfield described John Calvin ...With Calvin, pneumatology (the doctrine of the Holy Spirit) came of age, being founded squarely on the Bible ... Trinity is of the very essence of divinity for Calvin. It distinguishes God from all false gods. 'Unless we grasp these [three persons in God], only the bare and empty name of God flits about in our brains, to the exclusion of the true God.' When we think of God (or speak or pray), we must think of the triune God.'

In this article no mention is made of Michael Servetus.

PART 17

In Gerard DeGroot's book 'Dark Side of the Moon' about America's obsession with getting men to the moon, he writes, in his preface, that it 'was originally intended as an antidote to my last book, *The Bomb: A Life*. Writing about nuclear weapons left me depressed, cynical, forlorn, and scared.' I can share those same feelings after studying and writing about the dreadful things we have done to others just because they did not agree with our religious beliefs.

In the democracies of the world today no one is fined or imprisoned let alone burnt at the stake for not agreeing with the doctrine of the Trinity. Those fearful days have gone but the same mindset is still with us. Heresy is still a reality for many.

The October 2015 issue of Christianity Today (if I am wrong on the date it's because I've lost that copy) had, as its cover story, 'How to define Heresy'. Inside they highlighted the early Creeds as providing an effective litmus test to reveal who is a real Christian and who is the heretic. Of course, the one all-important teaching is the Trinity and if you can't subscribe to it then you become an untouchable as far as most churches are concerned. Although, it should be remembered, that particular doctrine didn't get on to the ecclesiastical statute books until the end of the fourth century.

The New Testament itself provides no explanation or defence of the Trinity and any controversy over it is never mentioned within its pages which points to it as not being an issue at that time. Anthony Tyrrell Hanson, who was Professor of Theology at the University of Hull, wrote in his book, The Image of the Invisible God: 'No responsible New Testament scholar would claim that the doctrine of the Trinity was taught by Jesus, or preached by the earliest Christians, or consciously held by any writer in the New Testament'. Unlike the topic of circumcision which Paul discussed at length or the eating of food that had been offered to idols which had been problematic for some.

Most people accept the Trinity as a foundational teaching of the Church. Others, because it's what they have been taught. There are those who have studied the subject and have been persuaded that it is a reality while others have equally been convinced that it is not true. Thankfully, no one is going to the stake for whatever religious position they take.

There are many divisions in the Christian community. Our beliefs can and do separate us from family and friends. This reflects the world we live in which is divided ethnically, politically and religiously. Perhaps we have been able to see in this short history of Christianity how radical has been the effect of antisemitism on the teachings and traditions from the early centuries onward. Paul wrote about a great division that was a live issue then, and is today.

This is the division between Jew and Gentile or as Paul calls it: 'the circumcised and the uncircumcised'. If we consider what he wrote concerning that division we can see how real and deep it is, but what we can also see is how the good news or the gospel can eradicate that wall of hostility and replace it with something much better and life changing.

We will find the problem, and the answer to it, in Paul's letter to the Ephesians. It might be best just to read it and then consider its content and implications. The version I am using is the TNIV. Eph 2.

11Therefore, remember that formerly you who are Gentiles by birth and called 'uncircumcised' by those who call themselves 'the circumcision' (which is done in the body by human hands) – 12remember that at that time you were separate from Christ, excluded from citizenship in Israel and foreigners to the covenants of the promise, without hope and without God in the world. 13But now in Christ Jesus you who were once far away have been brought near by the blood of Christ.

14For he himself is our peace, who has made the two one and destroyed the barrier, the dividing wall of hostility, 15by setting aside in his flesh the law with its commands and regulations. His purpose was to create in himself one new humanity out of the two, thus making peace, 16and in one body to reconcile both of them to God through the cross, by which he put to death their hostility. 17He came and preached peace to you who were far away and peace to those who were near. 18For through him we both have access to the Father by one Spirit.

If you are Jewish or non-Jewish, it makes no difference

before God because 'for all have sinned and fall short of the glory of God, and all are justified freely by his grace through the redemption that came from Christ (*the Messiah*) Jesus. God presented Christ as a sacrifice of atonement, through the shedding of his blood – to be received by faith'. Romans 3:23-25.

'For God does not show favouritism'. 'and there is no favouritism with him', Rom 2:11 & Eph 6:9.

It was the culture of Jews in the time of Jesus not to have any social contact with Gentiles. If they did they would consider themselves as needing a wash. Legalistic Jews would wash in a particular way and were critical of the disciples of Jesus when they were seen not washing before they ate. Jesus said to them that a little dirt isn't going to defile you, rather it's what comes out of you that defiles you. Peter refers to this separating between Jews and Gentiles when he spoke to Cornelius in Caesarea, Acts 10:28. As a result of this there was this wall of hostility between Jews and gentiles that Paul spoke of. See also Galatians 2:11-13.

These two sides – that are hostile to each other, are brought together as both are reconciled to God on the same basis – they recognised and accepted that the Messiah died that a new humanity could be created out of the two which brought peace to them as equals. 'through the gospel the Gentiles are heirs together with Israel, members together of one body, and sharers together in the promise in Christ Jesus'. 'Here there is no Gentile or Jew, circumcised or uncircumcised, barbarian, Scythian, slave or free, but Christ is all, and is in all'. Eph 3:6, Col 3:11.

When it says, 'by setting aside in his flesh the law with its commands and regulations'. It was not referring to the ten commandments or to the command to love your neighbour as yourself, but to the commands and regulations concerning the daily and annual sacrifices that were repeated endlessly year after year in the temple. Breaking in to Hebrews 10:9, we read, 'He sets aside the first to establish the second, and by that will (the will of God) we have been made holy through the sacrifice of the body of Jesus Christ once for all'. The laws regarding ritual sacrifices were, from that time, obsolete.

'Follow God's example,' Paul writes to the Ephesians in chapter five, verse one and two, 'therefore as dearly loved children and live a life of love, just as Christ loved us and gave himself up for us as a fragrant offering and sacrifice to God'.

'Just as people are destined to die once, and after that to face judgment, so Christ was sacrificed once to take away the sins of many; and he will appear a second time, not to bear sin, but to bring salvation to those who are waiting for him', Heb 9:27-28.

PART 18

Pilate had asked Jesus if he was king of the Jews and Jesus said, 'My kingdom is not of this world. If it were, my servants would fight to prevent my arrest by the Jewish leaders. But now my kingdom is from another place'. The night before, Jesus talked to his disciples about this world: 'If the world hates you, keep in mind that it hated me first. If you belonged to the world, it would love you as its own. As it is you do not belong to the world, but I have chosen you out of the world. That is why the world hates you … If they persecuted me, they will persecute you also … They will put you out of the synagogue; in fact, the hour is coming when those who kill you will think they are offering a service to God. They will do such things because they have not known the Father or me … I have told you these things so that in me you may have peace. In this world you will have trouble. But take heart, I have overcome the world … I am not praying for the world, but for those you have given me, for they are yours … I have given them your word and the world has hated them, for they are not of the world any more than I am of the world'.

In Paul's letters, this world is described as both dark and evil, and John writes, in his first letter, that 'We know that we are children of God, and that the whole world is under the control of the evil one'.

When Paul gave his defence before King Agrippa, he talked about what happened to him on his way to Damascus to arrest Christians as he was obsessed with persecuting them. He fell to the ground because of a blazing light, that blinded him, and he heard a voice that identified himself as Jesus, and he told Saul, as he was called then, to get up and stand on his feet. Jesus told him that he was sending him to the Gentiles to open their eyes and turn them from darkness to light, and from the power of Satan (Adversary) to God so that they may receive forgiveness of sins and a place among those who are sanctified by faith in me.

This is why Paul wrote to the Ephesians to be 'strong in the Lord and in his mighty power. Put on the full armour of God, so that you can take your stand against the devil's (Slanderer) schemes. For our struggle is not against flesh and blood, but against the rulers, against the authorities, against the powers of this dark world and against the spiritual forces of evil in the heavenly realms.

This is, and has been since the beginning, a dark age of violence, cruelty and oppression. This world is not going to end, but this evil age will. When Jesus was sitting on the Mount of olives, overlooking the beautiful temple that still had construction work going on, his disciples asked him, after he had said that all of the temple will be demolished, 'Tell us, when will this happen, and what will be the sign of your coming and of the end of the age?'

The first thing Jesus told them was to watch out that no

one deceives them because many will come, in his name, claiming that he, Jesus, is the Christ and yet will deceive many. He went on to say that they will hear of wars and rumours of wars, but not to be alarmed as these events must happen – the end is still future. Nation will rise against nation, and kingdom against kingdom. There will be famines and earthquakes in various places. All these, he said, are the beginning of birth-pangs. Then you will be handed over to be persecuted and put to death, and you will be hated by all nations because of me. At that time many will turn away from the faith and will betray and hate each other, and many false prophets will appear and deceive many people. Because of the increase of wickedness, the love of most will grow cold, but whoever stands firm to the end will be saved. And this gospel of the kingdom will be preached in the whole world as a testimony to all nations, and then the end will come … there will be great distress, unequalled from the beginning of the world until now – and never to be equalled again.

If those days, Jesus continued, had not been cut short, no-one would survive, but for the sake of the elect those days will be shortened … so if anyone tells you, 'There he is, out in the desert,' do not go out; or, 'Here he is, in the inner rooms,' do not believe it. For as lightning that comes from the east is visible even in the west, so will be the coming of the son of man … Immediately after the distress of those days 'the sun will be darkened, and the moon will not give its light; the stars will fall from the sky, and the heavenly bodies will be shaken.' See Isaiah 13:10 & 34:4) At that time the sign of the *son of man* (See Daniel 7:13-14) will appear in the sky, and all the peoples of the earth will mourn. They will see the son of man coming on the clouds of the sky, with power and great glory. And he will send his angels with a loud trumpet call, (See 1Cor 15:51-52) and they will gather his elect from the four winds, from one end of the heavens to the other ... but about that day or hour no-one knows, not even the angels in heaven, nor the son, but only the Father.

Someone asked Jesus, 'Are only a few people going to be saved?' Jesus didn't get into numbers but focused on how limited our own time is. 'Make every effort', Jesus replied, 'to enter through the narrow door, because many, I tell you, will try to enter and will not be able to. Once the owner of the house gets up and closes the door, you will stand outside knocking and pleading, 'Sir, open the door for us.' But he will answer, 'I don't know you or where you come from.' Then you will say, 'we ate and drank with you, and you taught in our streets.' But he will reply, 'I don't know you or where you come from. Away from me, all you evildoers!'

Jesus continued, 'there will be weeping there, and gnashing of teeth, when you see Abraham, Issac and Jacob and all the prophets in the kingdom of God, but you yourselves thrown out. People will come from east and west and north and south, and will take their places at the feast in the kingdom of God.' Darrell L. Bock, in his second volume on the book of Luke, puts it well when he says, 'the door is narrow *and* it will be shut soon. One must come God's way, and the decision needs to be made while there is still time ... Outward contact with the message and person of Jesus counts for nothing; inward reception is everything'. Pages 1236-1237.

It is believed by many Christians, and understood as coming from the words of Jesus himself, that those who are evil and unrepentant will suffer greatly and eternally in hell. This is not a biblical teaching but has been an ad-on and used over the centuries to scare people into becoming Christians. The word hell, often read in our bibles, is not a word Jesus used as it comes from the old English word *Hel*, goddess of the dead. The word Jesus used was Gehenna, derived from the Hebrew *gehinnom*, 'valley of Hinnom'. This particular valley had a dark history as it was used as place for child sacrifice (Jer 7:30-34 & 32:35) and by the time of Jesus it was used as a place to burn rubbish.

Many Christian teachers will quote Jesus when he said, '… it is better for you to enter the kingdom of God with one eye than to have two eyes and be thrown into hell, where their worm does not die and the fire is not quenched.'

That sounds very much like the picture of hell that is believed by many. But did Jesus really teach that there is a place where worms are immortal and those suffering in the fire will never die? These words were not original words of Jesus as he was quoting from the last verse of Isaiah which says: 'And they will go out and look on the dead bodies of those who rebelled against me; their worm will not die, nor will their fire be quenched, and they will be loathsome to the whole human race.'

Jesus may have pointed to that burning rubbish tip when he spoke of where the unrepentant will end up. All biblical references to people being burned up like so much rotting wood speak of it as being burnt to ashes; completely destroyed. That's what happens when combustible things are thrown into a furnace. See 2 Peter 2:6 & Malachi 4:1.

So what will happen to the evil and unrepentant people?

It needs to be said at this point that somehow everything that we do is recorded and kept – an unsettling thought.

1,000 years after the first resurrection and Christ's return, there will be another resurrection. This will involve all those who did not belong to Christ. They will be judged according to what they had done. Jeremiah wrote, 'I the Lord search the heart and examine the mind, to reward everyone according to their conduct, according to what their deeds deserve', later in Jeremiah's book, we read this: 'Your eyes are open to the ways of all; you reward everyone according to their conduct and as their deeds deserve'. Almost identical with the first quote and must be of importance for it to be repeated.

Much of that highly symbolic book, Revelation, has been mined from the Old Testament, as we will notice when we read about the judgment of the dead. 'Then I saw a great white throne and him who was seated on it. The earth and the heavens fled from his presence, and there was no place for them. And I saw the dead, great and small, standing before the throne, and books were opened. Another book was opened, which is the book of life. *The dead were judged according to what they had done as recorded in the books.* The sea gave up her dead that were in it, and death and Hades (the grave) gave up the dead that were in them, and *everyone was judged according to what they had done.* Then death and Hades were thrown into the lake of fire (no more death or the grave). The lake of fire is the second death. All whose names were not found written in the book of life were thrown into the lake of fire'. Revelation 20:11-15.

I cannot add to that except to repeat what Jesus said in what is called, the beatitudes: *'Blessed are the merciful, for they will be shown mercy'.*

ACKNOWLEDGEMENTS

I could not have written this short history without leaning heavily on real historians. I've pillaged, looted and torn my way through many books that had been gathering dust on the selves, and at times used more than one or two to get a fuller picture. The author's names and titles are below. Any mistakes are all mine.

November 2023

BIBLIOGRAPHY

Atherstone, Andrew, *The Reformation. Faith & Flames*

Bede, *A History of the English Church and People*

Bock, Darrell L, *Luke 9:51-24:53 Commentary*

Carroll, James, *Constantine's Sword*

Chandler, Kegan, A. *The God of Jesus*

Chang, Eric H.H. *The Only True God*

Childs, Jessie, *Henry VIII'S Last Victim*

Davidson, Ivor J, *The Birth of the Church*

_____, *A Public Faith*

DeGroot, Gerard, *Dark Side of the Moon*

Goldstone, Lawrence & Nancy, *Out of the Flames*

Foxe, John, *Book of Martyrs*

Fountain, David, *John Wycliffe*

Freeman, Charles, *The Closing of the Western Mind*

_____, *AD 381*

_____, *A New History of Early Christianity*

Hanson, Anthony Tyrell, *The Image of the Invisible God*

Holder, Meir, *History of the Jewish People*

Luther, Martin, *A Commentary on St Paul's Epistle to the Galatians*

Mills, Watson E. ed. *Lutterworth Dictionary of the Bible*

Mortimer, Ian, *1415*

Moyle, Franny, *The King's Painter*

Moynahan, Brian, *The Faith*

_____, *Book of Fire*

Nixey, Catherine, *The Darkening Age*

Pearse, Meic, *The Great Restoration*

Stephenson, Paul, *Constantine*

Wright, Jonathan, *heretics*

Reader's Digest, *After Jesus*

The History of Christianity, *A Lion Handbook*

Printed in the United States
by Baker & Taylor Publisher Services